THE
LATIN AMERICAN
TRADITION

THE
LATIN AMERICAN
TRADITION

ESSAYS ON THE UNITY AND
THE DIVERSITY OF
LATIN AMERICAN CULTURE

By CHARLES WAGLEY

COLUMBIA UNIVERSITY PRESS
NEW YORK & LONDON 1968

Charles Wagley is Franz Boas Professor of Anthropology and Director of the Institute of Latin American Studies at Columbia University. He is the author of *An Introduction to Brazil* and co-author, with Marvin Harris, of *Minorities in the New World.*

Copyright © 1968 Columbia University Press
Library of Congress Catalogue Card
Number: 67-30968
Printed in the United States of America

PREFACE

THIS book contains a series of papers and essays written between 1951 and 1964. All of them have been published previously but most of them are today not easily available. Some of them are republished here in their original form; others have been slightly modified for the present volume. These papers are unequal in length and varied as to the audience to which they were originally addressed. Chapter II of this volume, "An Introduction to Latin American Culture," is chronologically the earliest. It was issued in 1953 for the Foreign Service Institute of the U.S. Department of State as a document to be used in training government employees for service in Latin America. It appeared first in mimeographed form and then in offset print; and it has been used by a variety of organizations for training purposes. Occasionally it has been cited in scholarly works. This paper attempts to be light in tone, practical, and nontechnical. Yet in it some of my basic views of Latin American culture, which were developed later in more scholarly form, appear for the first time. The other papers in this volume were written for more scholarly audiences; they first appeared as contributions to symposia, to scientific meetings, or to scholarly journals. In many ways they are extensions and refinements of my thinking as introduced in the earlier "popular" paper mentioned above.

Despite their varied origins, it seems to me that these papers develop a consistent point of view in regard to Latin American society and culture. All of them are concerned with a set of traditions, institutional values, and patterns of behavior which are shared by most Latin Americans. In these papers, I have conceived of Latin America as a broad culture sphere set off in many ways from the Anglo-American culture sphere with which it shares the New World. Although it is fashionable nowadays to stress the dynamic social and economic changes underway in Latin America, I have stressed in these papers the persistence of traditional ways of thought and behavior patterns and their tenacity in face of fundamental social and economic change.

Finally, the papers included in this volume are concerned with differences and variations in Latin American society and culture. There are regional variations within the Latin America culture sphere that result from differences in environment, differences in the pre-Columbia cultures, and differences in historical formation under European rule. And, in every Latin American nation, there are internal cultural differences resulting from the different degrees of economic, social, and political integration of various sectors of the population into national life. By attempting to seek the universal or the common denominator in Latin American culture and by attempting to classify the regional and internal subcultures of Latin America, the papers in this volume hopefully present a framework for further research in Latin America.

In a book which contains essays and papers written at different times and for a variety of audiences, it is difficult to remember all of those people to whom one owes an intellectual debt. I am sure that my former students, research associates, and colleagues who have shared my interest in Latin American culture over the last decades will recognize their contributions and will realize my sincere gratitude. I do wish, however, to specifically thank Marvin Harris for his permission to include in this volume "A Typology of Latin American Subcultures" which was written in joint authorship with him. I would also like to thank Robert Tilley, Assistant Director of the Columbia University Press, who helped me select and encouraged me to edit the papers for the present volume. I am grateful to Fredrick A. Praeger, Publishers, to Stanford University Press, to the Foreign Service Institute of the U.S. Department of State, and to the Editors of the *American Anthropologist* and the *Proceedings of the Academy of Political Science* for permission to reprint papers which originally appeared under their imprint. I also wish to thank the editors of the volumes from which certain of these papers first appeared, namely Joseph Maier and Richard W. Weatherhead, Editors of *The Politics of Change in Latin America* (Praeger, 1963), and John J. Johnson, Editor of *Continuity and Change in Latin ·America* (Stanford University Press, 1964). I also wish to thank Mrs. Dorothy Psomiades and my wife, Cecilia Roxo Wagley, for editorial and bibliographical assistance.

Most of the papers in this volume remain fundamentally unchanged from their original versions, despite the temptation at this late date to make changes reflecting modifications in my point of view over the last decade. The papers do not follow a chronological order; I thought it best to let the papers expose the development in my thinking. Bibliographical references have been brought up to date and there are references in footnotes to research that has been undertaken since the publication of the original papers. The first chapter, "A Framework for Latin American Culture," was, of course, written especially for this volume; and I have made some substantial changes in

Chapter VII, "The Dilemma of the Latin American Middle Class," since the middle class and the elite are the subject of considerable on-going dialogue among sociologists and anthropologists interested in Latin America.

CHARLES WAGLEY

New York
September 1967

CONTENTS

THE
LATIN AMERICAN
TRADITION

A FRAMEWORK FOR
LATIN AMERICAN CULTURE

AFTER its discovery by Europeans, two separate culture spheres took form in the New World. In the north, and Anglo-American culture sphere composed of the United States and English-speaking Canada predominated; to the south, those countries originally colonized by Spain and Portugal (and the French and Spanish-speaking islands) came to be known as Latin America. Each of these culture spheres, Anglo-America and Latin America, represent distinctive adaptations of man to the New World. Within the boundaries of each of them, the American Indian, the African Negro, East Indians, Chinese, Japanese, Italians, Polish, Germans, and other peoples have been incorporated and have made important cultural contributions; but the mother countries furnished the basic social and cultural institutions. Out of their common experience in the New World, both Anglo-America and Latin America share many characteristics and problems which set them off from Europe and other culture spheres of the world. But Anglo-America and Latin America are fundamentally different. It is almost as if the cultural and social differences between sixteenth and seventeenth century Protestant, neo-capitalistic, and bourgeois-oriented northern Europe, and Catholic, semi-feudalistic and aristocratic oriented southern Europe became

accentuated in the countries they nourished in the New World.
The cultural differences between Anglo-America and Latin
America have been a barrier to understanding between the
peoples of the western hemisphere. Aside from economic and
political differences of opinion and interests, there have been
fundamental misunderstandings of each other's culture values,
ideology, and aspirations. The papers in this volume are attempts to understand, explain, and analyze such cultural
differences between Anglo-America and Latin America. Yet
the point of view in these papers is not explicitly comparative.
Rather, they focus upon Latin America, in an attempt to explain Latin American culture to Anglo-Americans. Such a point
of view, unfortunately, sometimes contains Anglo-American
presumptions; it often implicitly assumes a knowledge of
Anglo-America habits, behavior patterns, and institutions.
Nevertheless, the point of view is objective and attempts to
seek out some of the basic common features and fundamental
variations in the way of life of Latin America and to provide
an overview that often escapes Latin Americans themselves.

THE COMMON DENOMINATOR OF
LATIN AMERICAN CULTURE

As a result of their common Iberian cultural heritage and of
similarities in historical experience in the New World, a set of
traditional "ideal patterns" which guide the behavior of most
Latin Americans seems to act as a common denominator
through the whole culture sphere (Gillin 1947B; 1955). By
"ideal pattern," I mean "The consensus of opinion on the part
of a society's members as to how people should behave in
particular situations" (Linton 1945: 52). In addition, I would
like to extend Linton's concept of "ideal patterns" beyond the
realm of action in a given situation to include the models
which people have in their minds as to how an institution

ought to be organized and how it ought to function.* In other words, in my terms an ideal pattern may be the way the people of a society think that the family ought to be organized or it may be the way a man ought to behave in his role as father. It must be said at once that such ideal patterns are seldom to be equated with the behavior of people in any society. They are often articulated but honored in the breach when it comes to action. We are all aware that people do not do what they say they should. Yet ideal patterns, although often honored in the breach, profoundly affect the meaning of behavior. The practice of polygyny (multiple wives), for example, has an utterly different meaning in a society which holds polygyny as an ideal pattern than it has in another society in which one wife at a time is the ideal pattern. And I think that it can be predicted that in a society where polygyny stands as an ideal pattern, more men will have two or more wives than in a society that makes a single wife the ideal pattern. Yet it can also be predicted that in both kinds of societies, there will be some men with but one wife and others with several simultaneous mates (wives or mistresses).

The ideal patterns which are common throughout Latin America and which seem to me to profoundly influence the behavior of most Latin Americans are mainly patterns of behavior and institutional forms that derive from the Iberian Peninsula of the sixteenth and seventeenth centuries but that have been modified in their New World setting. They include familism, ceremonial and fictive kinship (the compadrazgo system), double standards of sexual morals, emphasis upon social class, a disdain for manual labor, high regard for formal

---

* I have preferred to use the concept of "ideal pattern" rather than concepts used by other authors such as "themes," "implicit premises," "ethos components," "values," and so forth because ideal patterns are more specific and concrete, although there is an obvious similarity between such concepts and "ideal pattern."

etiquette, an emphasis upon the saints and a love of display in religion (that is, religious processions and festivals), and other patterns of behavior and institutions (Gillin 1947B; 1955). Such ideal patterns of Latin American culture will be described and analyzed in the papers that follow, but it should be noted now that most of them are aristocratic patterns and derivative of the gentry.

This should not be surprising. It is well known that the early Spanish and Portuguese colonists did not come to the New World to do manual labor. They came to get rich, and either to achieve or to fortify their *hidalgo* or *fidalgo* (gentleman) status. They came to the New World to locate minerals or to secure land in the form of large grants. In some cases, they became exceedingly rich although often they failed; but almost everywhere in Latin America, an elite group was surrounded by servile Indians or African slaves who furnished them with labor and services. Almost everywhere in Latin America, the landed gentry dominated in the early centuries of colonial rule and established the ideal patterns to be emulated by others. As Robert Redfield has written: "The peasantry have been strongly influenced by the gentry or elite with whom their lives are completed and entertain views of what is good, desirable and ideal that have been taken over from examples provided by the gentry" (Redfield 1956: 130). In Latin America this was not only true of the peasantry but also of the businessmen of the towns, the minor bureaucrats, and the other lesser sectors of early Latin American society. In the colonial period, there was no solid middle class with its own ideology and values; the only model to be imitated by the mass of people was that of the landed gentry.

This did not mean, of course, that the peasantry, the workers on plantations, the minor officials in towns and cities, and even businessmen and traders could live up to the ideal patterns of the landed gentry. They simply did the best they could and held the ideal pattern as something that might be aspired to. But when a family moved up in the world, they tried to adopt the elite model set before them. Even the poor peasant or worker on plantation vicariously shared these ideal patterns. It was certainly impossible for a plantation worker (slave or free) or a peasant to avoid manual labor, but he could admire his *patrón* (boss or protector) who carefully avoided manual labor of any kind. In one way or another, the aristocratic ideal patterns inherited from Spain and Portugal and cultivated in the New World filtered down to all sectors of the Latin American population, except perhaps the most isolated Indian communities.

One of the striking phenomena relating to these elite oriented ideal patterns is their adaptability to the great variety of conditions within the New World. Throughout Latin America, in the highlands of Peru and Guatemala, on the pampa of Argentina, and on the islands of the Caribbean colonized by the Spanish, these elite ideal patterns took root in the national cultures despite remarkable differences in physical environment and historical events. In outlying and relatively isolated and frontier areas of the former Spanish colonial world, such as Paraguay (Service and Service 1954), and New Mexico in southwestern United States, the traditional ideal patterns derived from Spain became the models for social behavior and formed the social institutions. One of the miracles of history that seems to force the imagination is the strength of the impact of Spain on the New World in the first two centuries after its discovery. Despite the slowness and often utter lack of communications between the Americas and Spain and between one part of the Americas and another, Spanish institutions and Spanish popular culture were imposed upon Indians and Negro slaves in an amazingly short time. And in Brazil, despite its enormous size and wide variety of regional environments ranging from the tropical Amazon Valley to the semitemperate south, a variation of these elite ideal patterns, little different than those of Spanish-America, took form under Portuguese colonial rule.

These elite ideal patterns of Latin America nurtured in the colonial period have a remarkable resistance to change even under the impact of rapid social and economic change. Although many cosmopolitan Latin Americans will say that such patterns of behavior are "old-fashioned" and now a thing of the past, it is a fact that they continue to function, although often in a modified form, even in such modern metropolitan cities as Mexico City, Buenos Aires, São Paulo, Caracas, Lima, Santiago, and Bogota. In provincial cities and towns of Latin America they often function almost as they did in the nineteenth century. One would think that the exigencies of the urban scene in São Paulo with over four million people would require people to discard such elite-oriented ideal patterns. Certainly, the mass of people of São Paulo—the poor who inhabit *favelas* and the industrial workers—cannot live by, or even aspire to live by, these elite patterns. But there is overwhelming evidence that the São Paulo upper class, and even the upper middle class and the "new" entrepreneurial class are still much influenced by such ideal patterns. A study of Brazilian businessmen, mainly of São Paulo, finds them to be oriented toward traditionalist values. Familism remains important. Industrial enterprise is a family affair, and managers of factories and commercial houses are apt to be selected from among relatives or because of their loyalty to the family rather than for their managerial skills (Cardoso 1964). Even in the most modern Latin American nations, the strength of rural aristocratic ideal patterns continues to be felt. Solari (1964) found that the upper class even of the city of Montevideo was to a large extent composed of members of traditional landholding families; a study of the Argentine elite shows that they often derive from the rural *estancia*-owning families or, if they have moved up in the economic and social scale, they buy estancias, not only as investments, but also for purposes of prestige (Imaz 1964). And Arnold Strickon has shown the wide influence of family and kinship, not only among the working class creoles of the rural areas but also among the Argentine elite (Strickon 1962). In fact, it has been shown again and again that the persistence of these agrarian and elite-oriented ideal patterns provides a barrier to economic development, educational reform, and political modernization. (Cardoso 1964; Silvert 1961; 1967; Benjamin 1965; and Wagley 1963, for example.)

If the cosmopolitan upper class retain elite ideal patterns, then this is even more true of large segments of the populations of provincial cities and towns. It is true also of the new middle class and of the peasantry in the sense that they try to live up to such expectations (ideal patterns) within the realm of their social and economic possibilities. Even today a lower middle class Brazilian may entertain his foreign visitor far beyond the means of his miserable salary in order to live up to an ideal pattern regarding hospitality. And an Ecuadorian or Guatemalan peasant may go heavily into debt to sponsor a saint's festival even though he has been bombarded with more rational advice. The strength of these "old-fashioned" ideal patterns are apparent a hundred times each day in the life of any Latin American. This is to be expected. Any set of ideal patterns derived from historical experience and institutionalized in the religion, the family structure, the relations between socioeconomic classes, and in the educational system of a society will affect the behavior of future generations, even after such patterns have become outmoded. After all, it is in terms of such patterns that most Latin Americans were socialized.

By emphasizing the persistence of tradition in Latin America, I do not deny that most of Latin America is presently going through a dramatic period of social and economic change. I have written elsewhere about the drastic social and economic changes which have occurred in Brazil since 1930 (Wagley 1960). A paper in this volume, "The Dilemma of the Latin American Middle Class," discusses the trials and tribulations of this rapidly expanding sector of the Latin American population as the result of such changes. There is no doubt that Latin American nations, except for a few "backward" countries, are well along in the process of transition from an essentially rural, agrarian, and semifeudal type of society to an urban, industrialized, and technologically advanced type of society. And, in all Latin American countries, there are numerous individuals (businessmen, professionals, government officials, and others) who try to order their lives in terms of modern, rational, and pragmatic rules rather than by ideal patterns inherited from the past. As Kalman H. Silvert stated in a recent paper:

Significantly large groups in all but the least developed countries have become modern in outlook, although not as yet supported by an institutional order through which they can confidently and predictably work. The transitional nature of Latin American society can be seen in the co-existence not only of urban and rural subcultures and of European and Indian ethnic groups, but also, in the major cities, in the co-existence of those persons with the Mediterranean ethos [Iberian ideal patterns in my terms] and those who have—not the classically Liberal—but the more fundamental relativistic and partially secularist views of the modern civic pragmatist. (Silvert 1967: 52.)

If I have stressed traditional ideal patterns in this volume, I have done so to provide a "base-line," so to speak, for the changes that are now taking place in Latin America. I have also stressed traditional ideal patterns because they still provide a basis of common understanding among the people of diverse Latin American nations. Some of these patterns will undoubtedly disappear under the impact of what has come to be vaguely called "modernization"; but it is hoped that in the process much of the humanistic tradition of Latin America can be preserved. Modernization need not mean the loss of tradition.

LATIN AMERICAN DIVERSITY

A second broad theme with which the papers in this volume are concerned is that of social and cultural variation within Latin America. Once it has been established that Latin Americans have a firm basis for mutual understanding, then we must face the facts of the great differences within Latin America—from region to region, from nation to nation, and even between sectors of the populations within a single nation. So different are the various regions of that part of the Western hemisphere which we call Latin America from one another, and so varied is man's experience in them, that one sometimes wonders how Latin America can form a viable social and cultural entity. Although Latin Americans recognize today that they form a community of nations within the world order and although objective observers can state that in Latin America "there are probably more profound similarities among the countries than among any similar number of countries anywhere in the world" (Adams 1965: 279), the term and concept "Latin America" has not been used frequently within the area itself until recently. It was a term used more frequently in the United States and in Europe than in the South and Middle American countries. Although offered as a quip, there is some truth in Fred Ellison's statement that the concept of Latin America exists only in the United States where Latin American studies are pursued (1964:80). In fact Latin Americans seldom think of themselves under that rubric. Instead they think of themselves as, and quite correctly call themselves, Venezuelans, Costa Ricans, Peruvians, Brazilians, and the like. They do not consciously think of the ideal patterns which they share with one another but rather of the particular national characteristics and traditions of their own countries.

Spanish is the language of all the countries except Brazil and Haiti. Yet a favorite topic of conversation among Latin Americans drawn from different Spanish-speaking countries is the variations of that language as spoken in different countries. There are amusing, even socially embarrassing, different meanings given to the same word from country to country. A perfectly commonplace word in one country can be an obscene expression in another. Then, there are differences in accent and syntax such as those which distinguish the Spanish spoken in the La Plata region (Argentina and Uruguay) from that of Mexico, for example. And as Brazil becomes more and more a part of all Latin American gatherings (in the past it was isolated), there is the "problem" of Portuguese to contend with. Brazilians are amused when Spanish-speaking Americans call their language "Brasileño", the language of Brazil is Portuguese just as English is the language of the United States. Brazilians become somewhat irritated when their Latin American conferees state that they cannot understand, or even read, Portuguese. Yet language is one of the unifying forces of Latin America. Over almost a whole continent, although millions of people still speak indigenous languages, Spanish is the common language. And with a little effort and study Portuguese is easily understood by Spanish speakers; most educated Brazilians have little trouble understanding Spanish.

There is a world of difference, however, between the way of life of some Latin American countries and others. Highland Bolivia with its mass of Aymara and Quechua speaking Indians contrasts vividly with neighboring Brazil which is a vast lowland inhabited by people of three racial stocks. It would be hard to find two countries more different than Argentina and Mexico in terms of physical environment, archeological and historical past, and the composition of the population. Within the Latin American community of nations, one finds minuscule nations such as El Salvador, Costa Rica, and Panama along with gigantic Brazil. There are countries proud of their democratic traditions such as Uruguay and Chile and countries such as Paraguay and Nicaragua where democratic institutions are almost nonexistent. Some nations can boast of a high literacy rate such as Uruguay (80 per cent) and Argentina (86 per cent), while in others, such as Brazil (48.4 per cent) and Ecuador (48.9 per cent), more than half the population is illiterate.* It is not surprising that most books which attempt to generalize about Latin America as a whole tend to be rather superficial, sometimes vague, and full of caveats.

An eminent specialist on Japan was surprised when he was asked to look into Latin American studies. "In the first place," he wrote, "students of Asia tend to be more narrowly specialized. There are a few who take Southeast Asia as their oyster, some who bestraddle China and Japan, but most confine their research to only one society. By contrast, one hears of Latin Americanists but not of Bolivianists or Peruvianists" (Dore 1964: 229). Yet he found Latin America an excellent field for comparative studies. "Its societies do have so many points of similarity that an examination of their differences might yield new information about the way those differences are interrelated" (Dore 1964:229). Such comparative studies of Latin American societies and generalizations about Latin America would seem to call for a classification or taxonomy of Latin American subcultures, societies, nations, or communities. In

---

* Figures from *Statistical Abstract of Latin America 1962.*

making comparison, even among societies as closely related as those of Latin America, we must be certain that we are dealing with the same or different "species"—to borrow an analogy from biology. In other words, there must be some frame of reference that allows us to control the variables in comparison.

A specific example taken from the present volume will perhaps clarify what I have in mind about comparative studies in Latin America and elsewhere. In one paper in this volume, I have compared the peasantry of one Brazilian community with that of a Guatemalan community and drawn some generalizations from my comparison. Why did I select these specific communities (other than the fact that I did field research in both) in these particular Latin American nations? I might say at once that it seemed to me that the Brazilian community was representative of an "open *mestizo*" type of peasantry and the Guatemalan community was representative of a "close corporate Indian" type peasantry, and each was representative of a sub-region of Latin America, namely of Afro-America (Brazil) and Indo-America (Guatemala).

But such an explanation would be based upon a knowledge of taxonomies of subcultures and regions which are suggested in other papers in this volume. At this point I would have to justify my selection of the two cases of peasantry for comparison in more lengthy terms. Both the people of the Brazilian and the Guatemalan communities compared could be classified as Latin American peasants (or for that matter universally as peasants) in terms of their position in the national structure of their respective nations (that is, rural inhabitants who control the land they cultivate and who mainly plant for subsistence). As such, both groups are representative of a large sector of the Latin American population. But there are basic and crucial differences between the two groups, although both also share many traditional ideal patterns. The Brazilian peasant group speaks Portuguese, are fully aware of their identity as members of a nation, live in the tropical lowlands, own their land individually or squat on the land of others, and the content of their local culture is flavored by traits of African origin which the slaves brought to Brazil. The Guatemalan peasant group, in my comparison, are Indians in the sense that they speak Mam, an indigenous language of the Maya family, that they wear a distinctive costume which sets them off from the non-Indians of Guatemala, and that they think of themselves as members of an Indian community rather than as Guatemalans. Their local culture is flavored by survivals from their indigneous past which was that of the civilized Maya. Unlike the Brazilian peasants, they held land collectively. Thus, in the comparison of the peasantry of two Latin American communities, an attempt was made to hold certain factors as equal as possible, namely their Iberian heritage of ideal patterns and their structural and economic position within their respective nations, while the differences or variables between the two groups were made explicit.

It is for the purpose of intra-Latin American comparative studies as well as for purposes of comparison with similar processes and sociocultural forms in other areas of the world that social scientists dealing with Latin America have often been concerned with classification and taxonomy of internal sociocultural differences. Latin American national societies have been classified in numerous ways—in terms of degrees of urbanization or rurality, in terms of indices of "modernization" in their political processes, in terms of the size of the middle class, in terms of economic growth, and the like. Each taxonomy has its value in relation to the problem or problems under scrutiny. In these papers, I have been concerned in general with problems of Latin American social structure and culture as an anthropologist rather than with problems that generally fall in the realm of economics, sociology, political science, and history, although from time to time I might be accused of encroaching on other disciplines.

First, I find it useful to think of Latin America in terms of regions, each of which has a different type of physical environment, different ethnic composition of its population, and a different variety of Latin American culture. I have called these regions by ethnic terms, namely Indo-America, Afro-America, and Ibero-America (see Chapter II), but these terms are only symbolic. The basic characteristics of these regions do not derive from the ethnic or racial composition of their populations, although they do differ from one another ethnically. The fundamental characteristics of each region are the result of human ecology. Their basic social institutions developed from the interaction of man with the physical and social environment. That region which I have called Afro-America, for example, is not merely set off from the other regions by the presence of large numbers of people of negroid descent in its population. Instead, the fundamental differences between this region and the others were brought about by an institution, namely the plantation manned by slaves, and later by wage labor, producing cash crops such as sugar, coffee, and cacao, for a world market.* This institution flourished in the lowland tropics. Plantation life created a regional set of ideal patterns which persist throughout the region into the contemporary culture.

In a structural sense, it made no difference whether the slaves were African Negroes or people from another part of the world. They might have been Italians as many of the workers on São Paulo coffee plantations were at a later date. It was the position of the slave vis-a-vis the slave-owning planters and the economic system of the plantation involved in a sensitive

---

* I have elsewhere spoken of this region as "Plantation-America" and included southern United States as a part of the region (Wagley 1957).

world market that produced many of the essential characteristics of Afro-America. Yet, in another sense, it is important that a considerable portion of the population of this region derives from Africa. Despite the strong filter which slavery imposed on the transmission of African culture, African slaves were able to bring to the New World a remarkably large segment of their culture (see Herskovits 1941). The presence of an African cultural heritage fused with Iberian traits as well as the patterns produced by the plantation-slave-monoculture institutions give this region its distinctive characteristics.

Likewise, the criteria which I have used to characterize the other two regions of Latin America are both structural and genetic or historical. Both the structural relationships of various segments of the society to one another as well as the content of the cultural heritage are used as criteria. Thus, the criteria for establishing the Indo-American region include the structural relationships resulting from the exploitation of masses of indigenous labor (that is, *encomienda, repartimiento,* and other colonial institutions) by the Spanish minority, the presence of "free" Indian villages and haciendas, and other structural features as well as the persistence in the region of American Indian culture traits. And Ibero-America is characterized by the arrangements resulting from the presence of large numbers of relatively recent European immigrants vis-a-vis the colonial Spanish settlers as well as the culture patterns which the recent immigrants brought with them. Taxonomies based entirely upon structural models and ignoring the details of culture content are useful, in fact necessary, for broad comparative studies involving two or more areas of the world. But, within one cultural sphere of closely related cultures such as Latin America, variation and similarity of the cultural tradition also need to be taken into account.

Secondly, in my thinking about Latin America I have been

concerned with sociocultural differences within individual regional and national societies. The inner variation of Latin American societies need not be stressed because the tremendous contrasts between the modern cosmopolitian cities and the backlands of most countries have been described many times. Furthermore, the world is now fully conscious of the *favelas, barriadas,* and other types of slums and of the ultramodern buildings that are found in most Latin American cities. All social scientists feel uncomfortable about generalized statements about behavior in any Latin American society. What does it mean, for exmaple, to make the following hypothetical statement: "Brazilians are against foreign capital and industry." What types of Brazilians—the peasantry, the middle class, the students at universities, the São Paulo enterpreneurs and industralists, the politicans? Or, for that matter, does even a figure for the annual per capita income of say $361.60 for Colombia have any meaning without taking into account the distribution of such income among the various sectors of the population? Thus all social scientists—political scientists, sociologists, economists, and social anthropologists—need some sort of classification of the varieties of sociocultural sectors of Latin American national societies in order to reach meaningful generalizations.

Social anthropologists have particularly felt the need for some sort of frame of reference for controlling internal variation in Latin American societies. Since most anthropologists have undertaken their research in local societies, they have generally attempted to classify the types of communities or local groups found within a nation or they have tried to classify sectors of the national population along lines of cultural variations found within a region or nation. Only with such a taxonomy have they been able to make explicit what variety of the complex national culture is represented in their research sample (the local community) and how the local unit being studied relates to the more complex sociocultural national structure. The attempts for formulating a classification of internal sociocultural variation which are made in this volume have had in mind the research problems of the social anthropologists, especially those concerned with studies of contemporary local communities. Other disciplines of the social sciences might classify the internal variations of a complex national society by other criteria in a way that would be most useful for their particular research problems.

My first attempt at formulating a framework for internal variation in Latin American national society, which appears in Chapter II in this volume, was written in 1951 (but issued in 1953). It was a classification of Latin American community types. I was much influenced in my use of communities as the unit to be classified by the pioneer work of Robert Redfield. His, now classic, *The Folk Culture of Yucatán* (1941) distinguished four types of communities for the Yucatán Peninsula, although he stressed only the "folk" and the "urban" types. I was also influenced by Julian Steward and his colleagues with whom I had discussed community types at some length during the planning of the research that led to *The People of Puerto Rico* (Steward, Editor, 1956). They, too, used communities—as the units for their subcultural types of Puerto Rico. Their community types which were representative of insular subcultures were based upon productive systems (tobacco and subsistence crops, coffee, sugar cane) revolving around certain crops. My first attempt at classifying communities, which appears in Chapter II of this volume, was aimed at Latin America as a whole and it included a larger number of types than either the classification of Steward for Puerto Rico or that of Redfield for Yucatán. I distinguished tribal Indian, Spanish-Indian, peasant, colono (plantation wage workers), modern town and city types of communities. I used this community typology for some time in my teaching and in my writing about Latin America.

About the same time, I became involved in planning and directing a program of community studies for the State of Bahia in Brazil. Research was undertaken in three communities in the state of Bahia, each in a part of the state belonging to a different ecological region.* (Harris 1952, 1956; Hutchinson 1952, 1957; Zimmerman 1962.) It became clear in the process of research in these Brazilian communities that it was difficult to describe any one of them by one of the community types listed above. It was not that the community types did not describe cultural differences adequately but rather that each community was internally heterogeneous. In one Bahian community, there was a segment of the population which one might classify as "peasants" as well as a segment obviously composed of "town dwellers" (Harris 1956). In another Bahian community in which research was undertaken, four distinct population segments were present, namely peasants, colonos, town dwellers, and city upper class (who were also plantation owners). (Hutchinson 1957.) It seemed to us that there was more similarity in the variations of the national culture of Brazil exhibited by the peasants in all communities than between the peasants and the town dwellers in the same community. It became clear that a variety of the national culture, a subculture, which represented the way of life of a segment of a community was the unit to be classified. Although theoretically a community might be made up of but one subculture (Kottak 1966), most communities contained more

---

* Although not directly a part of this program, the research by Anthony Leeds (1957) in the Cacao Zone of Bahia State and the research by the present author and associates in the Amazon Valley (Galvao 1955; Wagley 1952 and 1953B) provided additional comparative data on the Brazilian community.

than one. Thus, in the paper which appears as Chapter III in this volume, Marvin Harris and I identify nine distinctive subculture types which appear in Latin American communities.

As in the division of Latin America by regions mentioned above, both structural and historical criteria were used to establish these subcultural types. Rural farmers, for example, producing mainly for subsistance but also for local markets are classed as peasants, and thus as carriers of a Peasant-type subculture. They are classed as peasants not only because of their economic situation and their particular relationship to town dwellers but also because the subculture which forms their way of life contains archaic Iberian traits fused with traits of Indian and African origin. Yet, in the attempt to generalize for all of Latin America and to provide categories for comparative studies among Latin American societies, considerable detail of culture content (historical criteria) had to be sacrificed in favor of structural criteria. Thus, rural subsistence cultivators of Haiti, Brazil, Peru, Guatemala, Argentina, and Chile were classed together as peasants despite the considerable differences in cultural traits present in each national and regional setting. To recognize fully the import of culture content, we might have identified at least three Peasant subculture types— an Afro-American Peasant subculture, an Indo-American Peasant subculture, and an Ibero-American Peasant subculture. The same would be true of the other subculture types; thus, we would have had to identify a total of twenty-seven types by combining the regional classification (which stresses history and culture content) with a classification which stresses structure.

Yet by including culture content in our taxonomy as well as structure, Harris and I differed from Eric Wolf who published in the same year a typology of Latin American peasantry. Wolf used structural criteria to the point of ignoring what seemed to us some obvious cultural criteria (Wolf 1955). In his category of peasants, he included both those people we identified as carriers of a Peasant subculture and those we had called Modern Indian, although he set off some Indians as a special breed of peasants on the basis of their system of corporate land tenure system and their "closed" communities. It seemed to us at the time, and it still seems so to me, that the Indians of highland Latin America and some groups of Indians in the lowlands, who are peasants by a structural definition, should be distinguished from other rural cultivators. Unlike other rural peasants, these Indians continue to speak indigenous languages, think of themselves as members of communities or of groups distinct from the nationals of the country in which they live, and, because of visible cultural symbols, such as dress, house-type, and the like, they are considered to be Indians by others.

Yet in any cross-cultural typology embracing several culture areas of the world, those people who are called peasants sometimes differ from the other nationals of their countries in language, village institutions, land tenure systems, and the like, as do the Indians of Latin America. In a later essay on the Latin American peasantry (Chapter IV), I included the highland Indians as peasants, but I made a basic distinction between Indian and Mestizo type peasantry in Latin America. Within Latin America, there is a fundamental subcultural difference between Indians and other rural cultivators which involves different patterns of expected behavior.

A FRAME OF REFERENCE IN OPERATION

Theoretically, whether or not any frame of reference or classificatory scheme will be of value to a developing science depends upon its utility in empirical research and its usefulness in ordering the resulting data. In the social sciences, such a conceptual framework should also allow for prediction, with reasonable accuracy, of the behavior of segments of the population. Furthermore, a frame of reference such as the one formulated in some of the papers in this volume should have an additional "pay off" in guiding further analytical and descriptive research. It should uncover areas of weakness and strength in empirical knowledge of Latin America.

It must be admitted at once that the regional and subcultural frame of reference proposed in this volume does not fulfill all of these ideal criteria for scientific utility for social science research on Latin America. Its shortcomings are more practical than theoretical. The units of analysis are not the units for which quantitative data is usually gathered. Statistics are available, in more or less reliable form, for nations, states, municipios, and other political units; these political units are not geographically the same as the cultural regions suggested in this volume. Southern Brazil, to cite but one example, should be classified culturally with Ibero-America (Argentina, Uruguay, Chile, and Paraguay), while northern Brazil is culturally more akin to the region I have called Afro-America (Circumcaribbean). And the statistical data for social differences within political units tend to follow economic and social categories such as income, occupation, religion, and the like. Some of this economic and social data is sometimes symptomatic of subcultural differences within a nation, but they can not be used to define national subcultures. The widely cited and highly useful classification of Latin American countries by the size of the middle class constructed by Gino Germani is a case in point. Using economic and social criteria such as the degree of urbanization, industrialization, literacy, education, ethnic homogeneity, and so forth, a segment of each nation is defined as "middle class" (Germani 1962). These criteria certainly show the varied strength of a middle strata in the various nations, but there is still some doubt whether such groups are, in fact, set off from others in their nations by cultural criteria—by a distinctive ideology, behavior patterns, and self-identity. It would call for qualitative studies somewhat along the lines of the anthropological community study to uncover attitudinal and behavioral regularities which would be diagnostic of a Latin American middle class. It is clear that social scientists must make use of other frameworks for research and theory for both strategic and sometimes theoretical purposes. A frame of reference applying structural and cultural criteria is not the only way of ordering Latin American data, and it may not be the most strategic for many social scientists.

Yet it seems to me that a subcultural frame of reference combined with a regional division of Latin America provides us with a most useful instrument for thinking about Latin America, although quantitative data may be unavailable within these categories. This is particularly true when one is working with data of the type usually collected by sociologists and social anthropologists using community study methods. The utility of such a frame of reference for dealing with social and cultural data is made amply apparent in this volume. The use of a subcultural classification was illustrated by Harris and myself in ordering the data on political behavior from various Bahian communities during the elections of 1950 in Brazil (Chapter III). In writing about social race (Chapter V), I found differences in the criteria for racial categories between Indo-America, Afro-America, and the United States (Ibero-America was not included in the comparison), which were historically conditioned. I feel certain that, if data were available, subcultural differences in establishing social racial groups would be discernible within each region of Latin America.* In

---

* Conrad Kottak (1966) in a study of a homogeneous lower class community in Brazil found significant subcultural differences in the application of categories of social race and in the form and function of kinship between the lower and the Brazilian middle and upper classes.

reviewing kinship within Brazil, I found differences in the size of kinship groups between the peasants, plantation workers, urban proletariat, and the metropolitan upper class (Chapter VI). And, in writing about the Latin American middle class, I sought consistencies in their behavior when faced with the problems of social and economic change which set them off culturally as well as economically and socially from the other classes (Chapter VII). As Arnold Strickon has shown, structural and historical typologies have been found most useful in ordering social anthropological data on Latin America since Redfield's early work almost a generation ago (Strickon 1964).*

As stated above, a framework for research can also be helpful in making an inventory of research needs and in seeking research lacunae. In the paper by Harris and myself published in this volume, certain obvious lacunae were noted, particularly the lack of studies of plantation and urban subcultures. Some of these weak points in our descriptive knowledge of Latin American culture are being strengthened, but there are still few studies of plantations (and haciendas) as compared to Indian and peasant subcultures. Oscar Lewis has published his famous studies of the urban poor in Mexico City (1959; 1961) and of poverty-stricken Puerto Ricans in San Juan and New York (Lewis 1966). Sociologists and anthropologists such as Andrew Pearse (1958), William Mangin (1965), and Anthony Leeds have undertaken research in lower class shanty town slums but to date there is no detailed monograph describing the internal organization and the life ways of a particular urban slum settlement. Cultural studies of the metropolitan middle class and upper class are in general still lacking despite the central role assigned to these subcultures in the process of social change in Latin America (Strickon 1964: 157). And if

* Strickon speaks of the typologies for Latin America developed by Steward and his colleagues (1955 and 1956), by Richard Adams (1956), and by Wagley and Harris (1955) as "evolutionary." I would prefer "structural-historical."

we look at cultural studies in regional terms, the only published community study available for the whole region of Ibero-America at this late date is that by Elman and Helen Service on Paraguay (1954).

One of the questions still to be answered is how such segments of urban societies are to be studied by research techniques which produce descriptions of their subcultures. Such segments of the population are not communities and community study techniques will have to be modified and undoubtedly supplemented by data, research methods, and concepts derived from other disciplines. The unit of research cannot be the whole community but some part of it. A suggestive strategy for social anthropologists and others interested in culturally oriented studies was offered by Arnold Strickon in his survey of anthropology in Latin America in *Social Science Research on Latin America* (Wagley, Editor, 1964):

In the attempt to understand the culture of the emerging groups in Latin America it will probably be necessary to attack the problem at a number of levels. The focus of such studies might be such phenomena as immigration, regional or national development programs, or power structure. On the other hand, studies might focus on such groups as voluntary associations, occupational groups or categories, and others that we know are critical to the organization of urban peoples in other parts of the world. Similarly kinship as a means of structuring economic and political elites might come in for study. A critical group in the economic or political life of the community might be isolated as the focus of interest. Then, the inter-connections both within and without the community of this group could be traced. The community would not serve as the focus of interest. It would be merely the stage upon which we could see the myriad of connections (both within and without the locality) among the people, their organization, and various categories of cultural phenomenon. This is no revolutionary suggestion (see Wolf 1956) but the actual attempt to carry it into practice is yet to be made." (Strickon 1964: 158.)

Examples of the type of research by anthropologists which seems to be suggested by Strickon are a study of factories in Mexico City now being undertaken by Charles Wilson and the study of Umbanda, a syncretic religious cult in Rio de Janeiro, by Diana Brown. In his research on factories, Charles Wilson (N.D.) has made use of community study techniques but the factory rather than the community has been his unit of research. The community (Mexico City) has been the "stage" to use Strickon's term, and he has dealt with at least three metropolitan subcultures—the workmen, the technicians and white collar employees, and the factory owners. In her study of a widespread religious movement which is essentially urban, Diana Brown (N.D.) has been dealing with individual "churches," some of which are lower class and others middle class in composition.[*] Likewise William Mangin's study of regional associations in Lima, Peru, focused upon a type of urban organization, but he was dealing with an urban subculture, namely that of the lower class migrant to the city about which we know so little (Mangin 1965).

An exceedingly crucial urban subculture for which data is needed is the elite. This segment of the Latin American society, as we have seen, has been important in forming the ideal patterns imitated by other groups, and yet our knowledge of the values, behavior and aspirations of the contemporary elite derive mainly from rather impressionistic observations gathered incidentally in studies of a more general nature. Among social anthropologists, only Hutchinson in his study of plantation community in Brazil (1957), Strickon in his study of the

[*] Both of these research projects will result in doctoral dissertations to be submitted to the Department of Anthropology, Columbia University.

ranching complex of Argentina (1960 and 1962), and Whiteford in his study of Popayán in Colombia (1960) have
provided us with some cultural data about the elite or metropolitan upper class subcultures.* Sociologists have become interested in the Latin American elite and have provided some
descriptive data (see Imaz 1964; Solari 1964). Yet our lack of
knowledge of the Latin American elite, of both the traditional
upper class and the new entrepreneurial upper class, is one
that needs to be filled by cultural studies. Cultural studies of
the elite would be of utmost interest and importance to students of political science interested in the power structure and
the political process.

But it is not just the lacunae in our data coverage of regions
and subcultures that a framework or a taxonomy can bring to
light. Once it is apparent that communities are internally
heterogeneous and composed of more than one subculture and
that such communities are in turn parts of a region or a nation,
then it is clear that studies must be made of the interrelationship between subcultures. Or, to put it more concretely, studies
must be made of the interrelationship of groups of people who
are carriers of different subcultures within the same local society as well as those who are carriers of subcultures which link
the local community with the larger society of which the local
community is a part. These interrelationships are important,
for as Ralph Linton put it, "The total culture consists of the
sum total of its subcultures *plus certain additional elements
which are the result of interaction.*" (Linton 1936: 275. Italics
my own.) Although most anthropological community studies
published in recent years have paid lip service to linking a

---

* Raymond Scheele is the only social anthropologist, to my knowledge,
who has carried out research primarily focusing per se on a Latin American elite, namely on Puerto Rican prominent families (Scheele 1956).
There is some doubt, however, if this managerial upper class of Puerto
Rico is typical of Latin America.

particular community to the national sociocultural system, few have actually demonstrated such relationships in any detail. Likewise, while many studies have distinguished the rural peasantry from the town dwellers within the same community, few have focused upon the lines of interaction between the two groups who live by different subcultures. Perhaps the most detailed attempt to link the local community to the wider and more complex sociocultural system has been the four community studies which appear in *The People of Puerto Rico* by Robert Manners, Eric Wolf, Sidney Mintz, and Elena Padilla Seda (Steward, Editor, 1956). Their studies were the result of simultaneous field research and much mutual discussion, and the individual community studies were buttressed by detailed documentation of Puerto Rican history and insular institutions. A few studies, mainly in Guatemala and southern Mexico, have focused upon the relationship between Indians and non-Indians (*ladinos*), and a recent study by N. E. Whitten (1965) for an Eduadorean town has treated the relationship of different "social races" within the same community.

As Arnold Strickon states in the quotation cited above, the notion to focus research on the interstitial elements which link subcultures is not new or revolutionary. Some time ago Eric Wolf proposed one highly suggestive concept, namely that of the "cultural broker" which, to my knowledge, has not been put to use in field research. A "broker" following Wolf (1956) is an individual who has an understanding of more than one subculture and acts as an intermediary between them. There are, of course, several types of "cultural brokers." The concept is further developed in Chapter IV dealing with the Latin American peasantry. Due to their relative isolation, the "broker" type is of primary importance in linking peasants to the nationally-oriented institutions and subcultures. Another profitable area of research which should reveal the relationships of groups of people living by different subcultures would focus upon institutions or organizations in which the different groups interact. In addition to factories, religious movements, and voluntary associations which were mentioned earlier, local and regional markets, where people of different subcultures and of different communities meet, often on more than economic terms, would provide data on the relationship of groups living by different subcultures (Mintz 1959). Furthermore such concepts as that of "networks" which are the lines of relationship of kinsmen, friends, associations, and even groups who interact with one another across boundaries of locality and social class, might usefully be applied in research in Latin America (Barnes 1954). In fact, related to this concept is that of Sidney Greenfield of "patronage networks" which he is now applying to Brazilian society (Greenfield Ms.). Such "patronage networks" derive from the well-known patrón-client relationship which permeates traditional Latin American life, and they act as social mechanisms linking local and national groups and institutions.

It seems obvious to me that within the next few years research by social anthropologists and other social scientists focusing not on the community as such but on the interrelations of groups, classes, communities, and subcultures will produce new insights into Latin American society and culture. Such research will need a framework of the social segments and the subcultures which in their totality and in their interaction make up the complex national societies and cultures of Latin America. Likewise, comparative studies within the Latin American culture sphere and between Latin American societies and societies of other areas of the world will require a frame of reference in order to control and isolate the many variables involved. It is hoped that the various papers brought together in this volume may contribute to this new perspective of Latin American society and culture.

[11]

AN INTRODUCTION TO
LATIN AMERICAN CULTURE

LIKE North Americans, the people of Latin America live in the New World. The necessary adaptation to this new environment has developed many common attitudes and customs which are the real basis for hemispheric solidarity. Each American nation has a European mother country: the Spanish-speaking countries have Spain; Brazil has Portugal; Haiti has France; and the United States and Canada have England. Like citizens of the United States, Latin Americans are Americans, and many of them do not like it when United States citizens preempt that term. Although all American nations derive a large part of their cultural heritage from Europe, all Americans feel that they are different from their European mother countries; and they are different. The experience of over four hundred years in the New World and the influence of other cultural heritages have increased the differences between the New and the Old World. The ways of life of North America and South America differ. There are differences in customs, in traditions, in institutions, in ideologies, and in individual attitudes and behavior patterns between the two Americas. These differences are sometimes marked and vivid, but they can often be traced to different emphases, variant interpretations

This paper was originally prepared for the Foreign Service Institute for training of overseas government employees. Issued in 1953, Foreign Service Institute, Department of State, Washington, D.C.

of a similar custom, or unlike functions of similar institutions. Such differences make it difficult for the people of North America to understand Latin America and vice versa. It is hoped that this description will be of some help in explaining Latin American culture to North Americans.

Three distinct cultural heritages—the American Indian, the African Negro, and the European—have fused into the fabric of Latin American culture. Three racial stocks—the Caucasoid European, the Amerind, and the Negro—have mixed to form its present population. The three cultural heritages have not blended equally throughout Latin America, and the three racial stocks are not present in the same proportion in the population of all regions. Everywhere European traditions predominate to form the basic framework of the way of life of each nation. An upper class of European origin has been dominant socially and politically for over four hundred years. The cultural heritage transmitted by Europe acts as a common denominator throughout Latin America. In one great region, however, American Indian patterns have had an important effect upon the culture; in another, African traditions are felt strongly; and in still another, Iberian influences predominate almost to the total exclusion of the other two cultural traditions.

Everywhere the Caucasoid is a common element in the population. In no sense is the racial composition of the population necessarily coincident with cultural traditions; yet in one region the percentage of people of Amerind racial stock is high; in another there is a high proportion of Negroids; and in a third, Caucasoids form almost the entire population.

Latin America may be roughly divided therefore into three great regions—Indo-America, Afro-America, and Ibero-America. The first of these regions, Indo-America, includes most of those countries along the main western Andean Cordillera of the continent: Mexico, Guatemala, the other Central American republics, Colombia, Ecuador, Peru, Bolivia, and northern Chile.* It was in this area that the Spanish conquistadors encountered complex native civilizations such as the Aztec, the Maya, the Chibcha, the Inca, and the Aymará. It was a region of relatively dense native population in aboriginal times. Mexico held over 10 million people and Peru over 6 million. In this region of Latin America, a handful of Europeans dominated a large indigenous population and attempted to force their traditions and way of life upon it. As usual under such circumstances, the conquered also influenced their conquerors. Today, there are over 16 million people in this region who are classified "Indian," while more than 40 million are classified *mestizos*, or Indian-white mixtures. The number of racially pure Caucasoids is relatively very small, and they are limited to a few restricted circles and families. In many of these Indo-American countries, Indian languages are used as much as Spanish, the official language. Several million people speak Quechua in Peru; at least a million and a half speak Mayan languages in Guatemala and Mexico; and Aymará and Quechua are spoken by more people in Bolivia than Spanish.

In these Indo-American countries, large groups of people who speak native languages, wear native costumes, and consider themselves to be a separate people from the nationals of the country are classed as "Indian." These Indians are Chamultecos (the people of the community of Chamula in southern Mexico) rather than Mexicans, or members of an *ayllu* (a social geographical unit among the Aymará and Quechua Indians) rather than Peruvians. Yet their way of life is not similar to that of the aboriginal American Indian, for during the four hundred years of domination by the Spanish and by

* This area corresponds generally to that called "Mestizo America" by John Gillin. (See Gillin 1949.)

Spanish-speaking nationals of the country, their culture has become hispanized. Even their native costumes are mainly Spanish in origin, resembling, in some cases, seventeenth-century lackey uniforms. They are at least nominally Catholic, although numerous aboriginal patterns have persisted in their religion. They have adopted European domestic animals and some Old World crops, although their own old crops are still basic to their agriculture. Their village administration follows old Hispanic forms impressed on them in the sixteenth and seventeenth centuries by their conquerors. European ritual kinship and numerous other usages and customs of European origin are important elements in their culture. *

Just as those who are classed as Indian were influenced by European culture, the way of life of the non-Indian in these Indo-American countries has been affected by aboriginal culture. This aboriginal culture is apparent in the language, which uses numerous indigenous terms in local Spanish, in the cuisine, which includes dishes of native origin made from aboriginal foodstuffs, in subsistence methods, in folk belief, and in handicrafts. In fact, the difference between many *cholos* in Peru, *ladinos* in Guatemala, and *mestizos* (as the simple non-Indian is called) of Mexico, and the Indians is often mainly subjective, simply depending on whether or not they consider themselves Indians or Mestizos. The way of life of the Indian and the Mestizo is sometimes almost identical in content. Intellectuals in several of these countries are leaders in an *Indigenista* movement aimed at raising the standard of living of the Indian masses and at pointing out the value of Indian traditions. There is a trend toward native (Indian) influences in art, and the Indian is being treated in literature. The pres-

* The term "Republican Indian" is sometimes used by anthropologists for such peoples living by Spanish-Indian culture patterns outside the orbit of national life, to distinguish them from the tribal groups still to be found in Latin America. (La Farge 1940.)

ence of complex native civilizations within large populations gives an Indian tone to this large region of Latin America.

In contrast, the region called herein Afro-America * received its distinctive cultural traditions from an economic institution, namely from the plantation using slave labor, and from numerous African slaves. Throughout the West Indies, the Guianas, a large portion of Brazil, and the lowland portions of Venezuela and Colombia, Europeans established plantations on which sugar and other commercial crops were grown. The aboriginal peoples in these lowland areas were relatively few in number and their cultures were simple in comparison to the Pacific highland civilizations. They were soon killed off by rapacious slave raids, by slavery itself, and by old world diseases to which they had no immunity; or they were driven back into inaccessible jungle.

For labor to operate their plantations, the European newcomers turned to Africa. It is estimated that more than 15 million Negro slaves were brought over from Africa; over 3 million came to Brazil alone. During the colonial period there were more Africans in this region of Latin America than Europeans. With the exception of the English and the Dutch colonies, slavery in Latin America differed from the form it took in the United States. It was brutal, as slavery was everywhere, but in Latin America several differences in slavery were important to later social developments. In these Catholic countries slave owners were enjoined by the Church to baptize their slaves. Once he had been baptized, the Negro slave was considered by the Church the moral equal of his master. Miscegenation did take place between Negro slaves and their masters in the United States, but in Afro-America it was more frequent

* In another place I have called this region of the New World "Plantation-America" and have pointed out the parallels with the deep south of the United States derived from the plantation-slave-labor complex. (See Wagley 1957.)

and more often publicly recognized. Iberians had little racial antagonism toward these darker-skinned peoples; the Portuguese especially confessed to a feeling of great sexual attraction to them.

The mulatto offspring of European masters and their slave concubines soon formed a distinct class of people. They were generally made freemen by their fathers, and in many cases Brazilian plantation owners sent their mulatto sons to Europe to be educated. In Brazil mulattoes entered the priesthood and the professions and they took an active part in government, commerce, literature, and art. A class of educated mulattoes also took form in Puerto Rico, in Haiti, in Cuba, and in other colonies within the region of Afro-America before the abolition of slavery. Furthermore, Spanish, French, and Portuguese law provided numerous ways for a slave to gain freedom (for example, by purchase or by service to the government), and even before abolition there was a large class of Negro freemen in all these countries. Once he was free, the Negro had the legal rights of a citizen, and many today take an active part in all levels of public life. Unlike the situation in the United States, a caste system of Negroes and whites did not evolve out of slavery in Afro-America. Miscegenation was continued in the area, and a large proportion of the present population has Negro ancestors.

On plantations during slavery, the cultural traditions of the transplanted Africans were subjected to constant acculturation. Although most of the slaves came from West Africa, several linguistic groups were represented; they were often forced to communicate with each other in a European language, or in a newly formed creole dialect. African languages survived only in small enclaves and for special ceremonial usages. As his language was forced to change, the slave was also forced to adopt the culture patterns of his master. But numerous African patterns have persisted. The European masters and the large class of freemen borrowed many African traditions from the slaves. Culture patterns of African origin are apparent in family organization, in food, in religion, in music, in folklore, and in other realms of Afro-American life. The Brazilian samba and the Cuban rumba, to cite only two examples from music, reflect this African background. In Haiti, in the Guianas, in Brazil, and in other places in this region, African fetish cults (the *candomblé* or *macumba* of Brazil and the voodoo or Vodun of Haiti) flourish. Far from being the mysterious and evil rites travel writers make them, they are continuations of rich, complex African religious forms integrated with the prevailing Catholicism of Latin America.

Not only the African traditions brought by the slaves but also the plantation system itself produced a set of cultural patterns distinctive to this region. The plantations usually produced one important commercial crop such as sugar. Monoculture is the prevailing form of agriculture even today throughout this region. The rhythm of work, the specialized tasks—in short the entire plantation system of production and marketing of sugar and other commercial crops—created similar social institutions throughout this area.

Each *fazenda, hacienda,* or *finca,* whatever the plantation is called locally, is almost a separate community with the owner's or administrator's house as its center. Many plantations have their own churches, schools, and stores to furnish commodities to the workers. Not long ago, Puerto Rican plantations had their own currency—small coins worth a specific amount only in the plantation store. The plantation provided a social system dominated by the aristocratic landowning gentry with specialized workers, household servants, and fieldhands forming successively lower social strata.

The third great region of Latin America consists of Uruguay,

Argentina, most of Chile, southern Brazil, and Paraguay.* This region is here called Ibero-America because in it the European culture has predominated almost to the exclusion of the other two components of Latin American culture. The indigenous population was exceedingly sparse in this part of South America, and the Spanish and Portuguese colonists were unable to afford the importation of many African slaves. The present population is thus overwhelmingly Caucasoid. The few Indians who survived and the few African slaves brought into the region during colonial times soon were absorbed into the Caucasoid population through intermarriage. Likewise, European traditions and culture patterns developed by the European in the new world predominated. Within this region lies the great *pampa,* the home of the *gaucho*—the cowboy of Argentina, Uruguay, and southern Brazil. Soon after the arrival of the European these southern plains were swarming with wild cattle and horses, the descendants of escaped European animals. Both the frontiersmen and the nomadic Indians of the region became famous horsemen. The gaucho, the frontiersman and his halfbreed offspring, lived from the slaughter of wild cattle, selling hides and allowing meat they were unable to consume to rot. As these rich lands became *estancias* (ranches), and as new breeds of cattle replaced the wild pampa cattle, the gaucho became a ranch cowboy. The old gaucho spirit—a spirit of bravado or daring, of swagger, of freedom of the pampa, and of antagonism to authority—continued. The

---

* Although Paraguay is often classed with "Mestizo America," research in that country by Dr. Elman Service indicates that Indian influences are more apparent than real. Although Guaraní, an American Indian tongue, is spoken by a large proportion of Paraguayans, and although a large number of Paraguayans boast Guaraní ancestry, the content of Paraguayan culture is overwhelmingly European. Even the so-called Guaraní music so popular in Paraguay is sung with Guaraní words to Iberian tunes played with European instruments. Furthermore, Paraguay has always been related historically to the River Plate region. (See Service, Elman Rand and Helen Service, 1954.)

gaucho became almost a national symbol of Argentina and an important theme in its national literature.

The most decisive European influence in this region, however, came in the late nineteenth and twentieth centuries in the form of Spanish, Portuguese, Italian, Polish, German, and other European immigrants. Argentina alone received more than 3,630,000 European immigrants between 1857 and 1948.* Less than half of these Argentine immigrants were Italians. Southern Brazil has almost a million people of German extraction, and many descendants of the Italians, Spanish, Polish, and Portuguese. These European immigrants were attracted by the rich lands of the pampa and the semitemperate climate that lent itself to the European style of mixed farming. In turn they stimulated the development of the region, adding to the European content of its way of life. Ibero-America is the most European and the most highly developed region of Latin America.

Latin American Community Types

Latin American society is one of great contrasts. In all three regions there are great modern cities such as Montevideo, Buenos Aires, Santiago, Lima, Caracas, Bogotá, São Paulo, Rio de Janeiro, and the City of Mexico where modern industry, advanced architecture, the latest fashions, and other aspects of contemporary metropolitan life may be found. There are also tribal savages who are still making war on encroaching frontiersmen. There are isolated Spanish-Indian communities living by aboriginal and Medieval Iberian culture patterns. There are communities of backward peasants similar to those found in

* Actually, 6,780,000 entered Argentina during this period, but in the same period, 3,150,000 left. (United Nations, 1948: 155.)

many out-of-the-way parts of Europe. Then there are settlements of *colonos* (plantation laborers) on large plantations producing sugar, coffee, cacao, and other commercial crops; colonos also live on extensive cattle ranches. There are progressive small towns, similar in many respects to small towns in the United States, which are closely related both commercially and politically to regional and national life.

These different types of Latin American communities, namely the Tribal Indian, the Spanish-Indian, the Peasant, the Colono, the Modern Town, and the City, reflect both economic levels of development and degrees of integration into modern national and commercial society. They also represent, in a sense, stages in the process of social change. It was the Tribal Indians who became Spanish-Indians under European domination. The Spanish-Indians become peasants as they lose their identity as a distinct "people" and are brought within the orbit of national society. Spanish-Indians (and Tribal Indians, too) became Colonos as their land passed into the hands of *latinfundiarios* or as they were attracted to settle on plantations as wage laborers. As peasant communities received education, more productive subsistence methods, and other benefits of modern Western technology, they became "Modern Towns" participating more directly in national affairs. Peasants, Colonos, and Modern Town dwellers migrated to Cities and thus became Latin American urbanites. This does not mean that these were necessary steps in social evolution. Spanish-Indian communities may change directly into Modern Towns. It does not mean that any one community fits exactly the abstract ideal of any community type. Settlements of Colonos on a model coffee plantation may have all the characteristics of a Modern Town. In Guatemala, peasant families (called *ladinos*) live side by side in the same town with Spanish-Indians.

A recognition of these community types can be useful to us

in understanding Latin America. First, there are basic variations in Latin American culture to be expected in accordance with the type of community in which one lives and works. Second, technical assistance in the form of public health, education, modern agricultural techniques and other basic reforms will stimulate the process of change from one type of community to another. It will make peasants out of Spanish-Indians; urban industrial workers and modern town dwellers out of Colonos and peasants.

Patterns of Latin American Culture

FIRE AGRICULTURE AND "GET RICH QUICK"

Despite cultural differences in distinct Latin American regions, and despite the wide contrasts within the way of life in almost any community, there are traditions, values, attitudes, customs, behavior patterns, and institutions that are common throughout Latin America except in the few surviving Tribal Indian groups. Most of these common culture patterns and elements are European in origin; many of them are medieval traits which have now disappeared in the Old World. Others of these common elements and patterns have emerged in the New World as a result of historical development since 1500. Many of the forms considered traditional and old-fashioned are now disappearing in modern towns and cities, and some are ideal patterns achieved only by a favored few although aspired to by most Latin Americans. Each of these common elements differs in accordance with the region and with the type of community in which it is found, yet together they provide a basis of similarity throughout Latin America.

The prevailing economic system of Latin America determines several characteristic patterns of Latin American society.

Although industrialization has been rapid since World War II, the economy of Latin America is still essentially based on agriculture. The people who live in Spanish-Indian and Peasant communities are mainly farmers. Furthermore, a large number of people work on commercial plantations producing sugar, coffee, bananas, cacao, and other crops for distant markets. In addition to agriculture, extractive industries such as mining and petroleum are important to the national economy of many Latin American nations. In only a few limited areas, such as Costa Rica, Antioquia (Colombia), and southern Brazil, small farms are worked by the farmer owners and their families. It is a system which combines subsistence and commercial farming in the way many North American farms do. Monoculture and extractive industry are the mainstays of the Latin American economy.

This emphasis on commercial farming and on extractive industries, both of which furnish raw materials for world markets, is disadvantageous to Latin Americans under present circumstances; furthermore, it leads to a very characteristic Latin American attitude. Regions depending mainly on monoculture and the production of raw materials are usually economically unstable. Prices for these products are exceedingly vulnerable to fluctuations in the world market. There are therefore periods of great prosperity and periods of intense depression. Most Latin American nations are thus characterized by "boom and bust" economies. Brazil, for example, has seen several major booms based on a short-term demand for one agricultural or extractive product. There was the sugar boom during the sixteenth and seventeenth centuries when Brazil had almost a monopoly on the world market; it was followed by gold in the seventeenth and eighteenth centuries; by wild rubber from about 1880 to 1912; and by coffee during the present century. Following each boom there was a collapse in the market and temporary economic disaster. Gyrations of world prices and demands affect cacao in Ecuador and Brazil; henequen in Yucatan; bananas in the Caribbean countries; sugar in Puerto Rico, Cuba, and other countries; and the condition of the Chilean nitrate industries, Bolivian tin, and Venezuelan petroleum.

One of the results of this economic instability is, therefore, this characteristic "boom and bust" attitude throughout Latin America. It is a desire to "get rich quick"; to make a strike by speculation, manipulation, or gambling; and to make a high profit before price levels crumble. Latin American businessmen have traditionally not been interested in a stable business built up over a number of years and based on a small margin of profits. Middle class urbanites do not look forward to a comfortable old age by saving a little bit each year, instead they hope for a lucky break—to win at the lottery, to gain special favor from an important government official, or to benefit from another windfall. People know from past experience that wealth comes quickly and that a sudden turn of events may bring near poverty again. Latin America is full of cities and communities once prosperous, but now poor. The richly ornamented churches of Bahia in Brazil attest to wealth once derived from sugar; the mines of Peru, Bolivia, and Mexico paid for the colonial buildings scattered throughout these countries; and the gingerbread and rococo mansions of Belem and Manaus remind people of the short period during the rubber boom when the Amazon Valley was rich from "black gold."

These countries were explored and settled by men anxious to strike it rich, not by stolid pioneers looking for land to work with their own hands. Cortez, Pizarro, Alvarado, and other well-known conquistadors came to the New World looking for gold and other sources of wealth. The Portuguese-Brazilian *bandeirantes* (flag bearers), whose expeditions crisscrossed regions still "unexplored" or "uninhabited," went after precious stones or slaves. The "get rich quick" tradition of Latin America dates back to the first century of the European period; the Iberians brought this ideal with them to the New World.

Most communities of Spanish-Indians and peasants do not share this "boom psychology," although they often feel the effects of economic trends. Many Spanish-Indians and peasants work during part of the year for wages. In Guatemala the coffee fincas depend on Spanish-Indians as temporary labor for harvest, and many Spanish-Indians and peasants are miners in Bolivia and in Peru. But in the main, Spanish-Indians and peasants are subsistence farmers outside the mainstream of the national economy. Their agricultural methods are similar throughout most of the areas of Latin America. These methods are borrowed mainly from the American Indian, though today they are improved by the addition of a few European crops and iron tools. The ox and the wooden plow were introduced by Europeans, but they were adopted only in limited areas and by a small number of people.

The majority of Latin American subsistence farmers are hand agriculturalists working with tools such as machetes (bushknives), axes, hoes, digging sticks, and spades. Their system of cultivation is usually slash and burn—or fire agriculture, as it is more often called—in which a garden site is cut from virgin forest, from high second growth, or simply cleared from a field which has lain fallow for some time. The brush and trunks are burned off after they have been cut down. Fields cleared in this way have limited fertility; after two years or more a plot is abandoned, or at least allowed to lie fallow for a few years. As a result, each year a large proportion of the available land is out of production, having been used recently for gardens. A Guatemalan Indian farmer feels that one third of his meager mountainside land must always lie fallow.

In lowland South America great tracts of forest have been cut away and burned for garden plots, and large areas of low second growth are considered unsuitable for farming by the people. The crops grown on these farms are mainly maize, manioc, yams, potatoes, and other native American plants. Neither the well-kept mountainside corn fields of Guatemala and Mexico nor the tangled manioc plantations of lowland South America produce much more than the immediate needs of the farmer and his family.

Furthermore, there are few domesticated animals on these peasant and Indian farms. Many farms have a few chickens, but they are so wild that they lay their eggs in the brush and are almost impossible to catch. Sometimes there are a few pigs, a few sheep, and other animals, such as llama and guinea pigs in Peru, but almost everywhere meat is a luxury. Almost no one keeps a milk cow; milk is seldom consumed. Tortillas and beans in Central America and Mexico, rice in lowland South America, manioc flour in Brazil, yams and sweet manioc in the Caribbean, potatoes in Peru and Bolivia, and other starches form the basic elements of the Spanish-Indian and peasant diet. Beans provide necessary proteins and help to make up for the lack of meat.

Unlike North American farmers, Latin Americans rarely have vegetable gardens and fruit trees to supply their tables with a variety of home-grown foods. Meat and fish are salted and dried in the sun. Potatoes in Bolivia and Peru are frozen to make *chuna*. Manioc flour and dried corn may be kept for long periods, but in general Latin American farmers have few methods of preserving foods.

Nothing resembling the canning of North American rural housewives or the smokehouse for the preservation of meats is found in Latin America. For the most part, people eat what they have when it is in season. They thus have austere periods between harvests when their meals are limited to a few basic foods. Mechanical aids of both traditional farming methods and modern gadgets and machines are also absent on these Spanish-Indian and peasant farms. Hand churns to make butter and manual pumps, for instance, are seldom seen. The many and varied farm implements listed in Sears Roebuck or a Montgomery Ward catalogue are mostly unheard-of luxuries. People do their marketing and shopping at weekly or fortnightly markets held in many peasant and Spanish-Indian communities, buying only a few manufactured articles produced by modern industry.

In terms of a national economy, peasant and Spanish-Indian farmers are "economic zeros," neither producing nor consuming products of the national commercial system. As transportation is improved, as agricultural techniques, instruments, and knowledge are introduced, and as educational facilities are made available, the needs and demands of the peasant and Spanish-Indian communities will increase. They will widen their basis of subsistence products and begin to produce for national markets as did the coffee farmers of Antioquia in Colombia and Costa Rica, and the small farmers of southern Brazil. As the change takes place, they will become producers of basic foodstuffs for the nation and customers for the growing industry. It is important to the economic development of Latin America both to bring these subsistence farmers into the national economy and to establish a more modern and diversified system of commercial agriculture which would not only provide food for its rapidly growing population but would also supplant the present "get rich quick" exploitation of the soil.

THE PLAZA PLAN

From the Rio Grande to southern Argentina, the appearance of Latin American communities is quite similar. Both the Spanish and the Portuguese had specific plans for the new towns and cities which were established in the New World. The Spanish *Laws of the Indies* gave detailed instructions as to how the new communities were to be laid out. The Portuguese, characteristically less precise in their colonial plans, simply attempted to form communities after patterns known at home. The similarity of most old towns and cities in Latin America attests to the success of the Europeans in carrying out city and town planning. Anyone who has traveled in Latin America soon knows what to expect. The towns are often built on a rectangular plan radiating out from a central plaza (a town square) on which the principal church, most administrative buildings, and the most important commercial houses are located. Traditionally, the best place to live is near the plaza. Away from the plaza and on the edges of town are the less-favored districts. But sometimes the terrain did not allow strict adherence to the "plaza plan" for a settlement, and occasionally, as in Brazil, the colonists and the native population did not closely follow the instructions of the colonial administrators. As Latin American towns grew, other plazas were added, and additional radiating streets complicated the simple one-plaza town. Thus although most Latin American towns built in the colonial period essentially follow a plaza plan, local circumstances often required variations of this basic arrangement.

Designers of these old Latin American towns planned narrow streets for use by pedestrians, a few carriages, and animal transportation—not for automobiles. Houses built flush to the streets offered a solid front to a person passing by. Houses were oriented inward toward a patio on a walled backyard (called the *quintal* in Brazil). As one enters these old Latin American homes, it is apparent that the family lives near the patio or backyard away from the street. First there is a small, seldom-used formal room to receive visitors. Intimates immediately pass along to the large dining room where the family is most likely to congregate. Since these houses are built against other houses on two sides, windows either face inward onto the patio or the backyard or outward onto the street. Many bedrooms have no windows, both because of the floorplan of the house and because people fear the night air which is thought to carry malaria and other ills. Sanitary facilities, when available, were installed long after the house was built. Water for many of these traditional Latin American houses comes sometimes from a public fountain or from a public well. It is transported in a jar by a servant or in wooden kegs by a burro. The kitchen generally lacks most of the modern facilities taken for granted in North America. Conveniences such as hot running water, a white enamel stove, and modern kitchen gadgets are not to be found. Cooking is done over an adobe platform stove which burns wood or charcoal; water is kept in large earthenware crocks.

These traditional homes are charming to visit. They are well adapted to the climate, except in regions where cold snaps indicate the need for some form of heating. They were constructed to house large families who led an expansive way of life.

Modern influences are changing both the physical appearance of Latin American cities and towns and the housing. Most peasants and Spanish-Indians still live much as they always have. Their villages, which were established by missionaries and colonial administrators, usually follow the "plaza plan," but their homes are simpler and smaller than the traditional Latin American dwellings described briefly above. The Spanish-Indians and peasants live in homes that are constructed of adobe, stone, straw, and palm thatch.

Many Latin American towns have changed because of the

modern roads that connect them more closely to the outside world. The stretch of road passing through the town becomes an important street. This street is often widened for automobile traffic. It becomes the town's principal *avenida*, like the main street of an American town—a development that is followed by the rise of new commercial houses and modern buildings. The plaza loses its importance as the center of town. Sometimes new "suburban" districts—with superior dwellings and even a small nucleus of commercial establishments—spring up on the edge of town. In these towns people build bungalows and other "modern" homes. They tend to set them back from the street and to leave a space between each house for side windows. These new homes have up-to-date sanitary facilities, running water, and other improvements. They also have lower ceilings, smaller rooms, and more exposure to the strong sun of the semitropical climate. In cities crowded conditions have created slum areas such as the infamous *favelas* of beautiful Rio de Janeiro. In the great cities of Latin America, the majority of the people live in modern apartment houses, in enormous housing projects, and in other types of newly constructed dwellings. As modern methods of transportation have been introduced, wide avenidas have replaced narrow cobblestone streets in most Latin American capitals. However, in these old cities the traditional plaza plan is still discernible; off the avenidas it is still pleasant to wander through small plazas where the old houses are flush to the sidewalk.

Neither the Spanish nor the Portuguese, however, were entirely successful in making townspeople of the native population or even of the European colonists. In colonial Brazil the early governors complained bitterly about their people's preference for living in scattered homesteads in the forest and near their fields. The Spanish carried out an energetic, sometimes brutal campaign (the so-called *congregacion*) to concentrate the dense native population of Indo-America into towns and villages. The many "empty villages" throughout Mexico and Guatema and other sections of Indo-America, in which the towns consist of nothing but a plaza and a few streets, indicate how often the campaign was unsuccessful. These empty villages contain a church, several public buildings, perhaps a schoolhouse, a few ceremonial houses, and a few residences. The majority of the community's population live scattered in the rural zone as do many North American farmers. The town is a religious, political, and market center to which people come periodically, just as they came to their ceremonial centers in aboriginal times. Unlike most Europeans, they are not town or village dwellers who go out each day to till their fields, returning to their villages at night.

LUNCH AT HOME

Like the physical appearance of their towns and cities and the architecture of their homes, Latin American diet and food habits are changing under the impact of close relations with the modern world. Mention has already been made of the foods raised and eaten by Spanish-Indian and peasant farmers. The meager content of their diet differs according to the locally available foods. Aboriginal and African dishes and diet habits continue to be widespread in Latin America. The food of the middle and upper class townspeople, however, is mainly European. It is characterized, if not by its dietary excellence, by its variety and quantity. A meal may include many plates and courses: sometimes a soup, fish, meat, vegetables, perhaps a salad, and one or more desserts. Rice is often eaten in place of the potato in North American meals, and fresh vegetables are less often a part of a meal. Meal hours and the content of meals differ from those we are accustomed to in North America.

Breakfast comes whenever you want it, but it consists only of coffee with hot milk and some bread and butter. Lunch is eaten at midday or one o'clock (as late as two or three o'clock in Mexico); it is a heavy meal made up of several courses. Dinner in Spanish-speaking countries is served late as it is in Spain, sometimes around nine P.M. In Brazil the dinner hour is usually earlier—about seven P.M. Throughout Latin America, both lunch and dinner can be long-drawn-out events. People like to linger over their meals.

A striking example of the persistence of a culture pattern in spite of functional demands for change is the continuation, in many Latin American metropolitan centers, of the habit of taking the midday meal at home. Modern business hours and modern bureaucracy call for a nine-to-five working day. Transportation problems are myriad in most Latin American cities. Yet cars jam the streets and people line up to catch public transportation—not just twice a day, at the beginning and end of business hours, but four times a day because they go home for lunch. Businessmen and officials protest that they are forced to go home for lunch because of the lack of adequate restaurants. Middle class citizens complain that they cannot afford to eat outside their homes. But midday meal at home continues to be a Latin American custom resistant to change in the face of adverse conditions.

Modern influences, however, are bringing changes in both content and duration of Latin American meals. Nowadays the North American in Latin America can often get a substantial breakfast even in a small boardinghouse or hotel. In modern towns and cities, the midday meal is simpler and more abbreviated than it was a generation ago. Many businessmen and public officials are forced to lunch in restaurants. Cafeterias and lunch counters can now be found in almost any Latin American city. The increased tempo of life and the transportation difficulties make it hard to have lunch at home. The hour of the evening meal tends nowadays to be somewhat earlier due to the pressure of new forms of entertainment such as the cinema. Only the rich can afford elaborate meals, not only because of inflationary food prices, but also because of the domestic help which such meals require. But on many plantations and in towns and cities in the more isolated areas, the table in the homes of the upper class is always set for extra guests—relatives or friends who arrive unannounced for lunch or dinner. The meals in these homes reflect the propensity of the Latin American upper class for luxury.

SOCIAL CLASS, NOT RACE

A rigid system of social classes has always been characteristic of Latin America. Although modern developments are beginning to modify class alignments, the traditional Latin American class system must still be understood by any outsider who hopes to participate in Latin American society and to comprehend something of Latin American culture. The structure of social classes in Latin America is apt to be confusing to North Americans, whose culture stresses social equality yet makes social distinctions based on race. Latin American social classes took form during the colonial period, and they persist into the present. Class membership is not based on one's biological race, but physical features are strong indicators of class position. It is a rule of thumb throughout Latin America that the darker one's skin color the lower one's social position and, conversely, the lighter one's skin color the higher one's social position. It is also true that prejudice and discrimination against the Negro and the Indian exist in Latin America, but they are milder and the form they take is different from that which we know in the United States.

Until late in the nineteenth century, Negroes and Indians were slaves, debt-bound peons, or "savages" living outside the orbit of national affairs. Slavery was abolished, and peons were relieved of their debt bondage, but the descendants of former slaves or peons entered the life of the nation with an indelible stigma. Their skin color and other physical characteristics indicated that their ancestors were slaves, peons, or "savages." Furthermore, these non-Europeans and their mixed descendants entered national life at the bottom of the social and economic ladder—as poor farmers, plantation laborers, servants, and other menials. During the late nineteenth century and into the twentieth century, educational facilities and possibilities for economic advancement were lacking in Latin America. Even though people of Indian and African descent theoretically have been granted equality of opportunity, they have not been able to improve their lot. In general, these "colored" groups are still the lowest element in the Latin American class hierarchy. Richer, educated Latin Americans look down on them as the poor, uneducated masses.

This does not mean, however, that there are any immutable barriers to social ascension in Latin American society because of one's biological race. Large numbers of descendants of Indians and Negroes have risen socially and economically in Latin America. In Afro-America, especially in Brazil, many individuals of Negro ancestry are active in public life and economic affairs. Important figures in politics, literature, art, science, and other fields of endeavor are frequently Negro or mulatto. Individuals of Indian ancestry are equally important in Mexico, Peru, Ecuador, Bolivia, and Paraguay. Many of these people are proud of their "Indian blood" (in Mexico it is said to be a strong political asset), and many Brazilians make a point of their mulatto status. Furthermore, such individuals are socially accepted; they move freely in the upper social and official circles.

Successful individuals with Negroid or Amerind physical characteristics are seldom thought of as mulattoes or Indians. Latin Americans think of an "Indian" as a person who speaks an Indian language, who wears sandals, and a quaint costume, and who is a poor subsistence farmer. It is not logical, therefore to classify a man as an Indian who speaks elegant Spanish and perhaps fluent French, who has a degree from a university, and who has florid manners and refined European tastes—even though he has the physical features of an Indian. Likewise, how can one classify a professional man who happens to have Negroid physical features with the illiterate Negroes and mulattoes? Such people, despite their physical features, are part of the Latin American upper and middle classes. In Latin America biological race reflects social position, but it does not determine it. Latin Americans tend to overlook those physical features of a person which do not correspond to that person's social position—to overlook Negroid or Amerind physical characteristics in wealthy and well-educated individuals. A popular saying in Brazil states the situation bluntly: A rich Negro is white and a poor white is a Negro.

Yet social classes are still rigidly separated in Latin America. In colonial times a small group of landed gentry dominated the great mass of Indians, Negroes, mestizos, and mulattoes. Today in some countries, the descendants of these colonial aristocrats—members of "good families"—still dominate the nation economically, politically, and socially. In many cities and modern towns, however, a new group composed of small government employees, businessmen, and members of the professions has appeared. In a few areas descendants of recent European immigrants have risen to supplant the old rural aristocracy as economic and political leaders. But there is some doubt in the minds of many students of Latin American society that this new group forms a "middle class."*

Rather, it is pointed out; these people who have climbed socially and economically out of the inert mass tend to identify themselves with the aristocracy. They adopt aristocratic values and imitate aristocratic behavior. The upper class tries to live up to what Gilberto Freyre, the famed Brazilian social historian, calls the "Gentleman Complex." Just as manual labor was the lot of slaves, peons, and Indians in the past, today it is considered the work for the lower classes. The upper and even the middle class prefer white-collar jobs at any cost. This group feels disdain for those aspects of professional occupations which involve physical labor. It is sometimes difficult to gets Latin American professionals to perform so-called field jobs. They prefer to administer, to plan, and to direct others.

Many Latin Americans are now doing difficult technical field jobs—wading through swamps, caring for patients in hospitals, and fighting diseases in rural districts—but these technicians are still exceptional. Most technicians want to work in the big cities in positions of direction. They want to be "gentlemen" in keeping with their upper-class status. Like other members of the upper class they do not like to carry bundles or packages. They even expect and receive special treatment before the law. Members of the lower class expect this behavior from the upper class. They often feel uncomfortable when a North American visitor insists on carrying a package or participating in manual labor.

* The Pan-American Union, Department of Social Affairs, published some time ago a series of studies concerning the "Middle Class in Latin America." Many of the essays and monographs which have been published in this series began or concluded by indicating the limited influence of the group which might be called the "Middle Class" in these countries. (Crevenna, Editor, 1950.) See Chapter VII for a later discussion.

All Latin Americans are very conscious of social ranking. From the viewpoint of an outsider, an Indian community might appear to be a homogeneous group of lowly Indians and a peasant village might look like a humble community of poor farmers divided by few social differences. But once one knows an Indian or peasant community from the inside, it is soon apparent that great differences in status exist. These communities distinguish between "rich" and "poor," although differences in wealth might seem small. A few outstanding men and women lead religious associations and belong to community councils. Certain individuals have great stores of knowledge about subjects such as religion, hunting, or agriculture. Others have special personal capabilities to cure the sick, to predict the future, or to assist at childbirth. Among workers on a plantation, there are differences in status between the "lowly" field-hands and the specialized workers. Each community has its own system of social rank which is recognized by the people of the community.

Furthermore, in Latin America people still admire the audacious, ostentatious, aristocratic leader. The ideal of the brave adventurer who came to the New World to become a "leader of men" still persists. The plantation worker often admires his patrón (employer) whose extravagance may be the cause of the workman's misery; the peasant is loyal to a merchant who he knows charges exorbitant prices; labor and political leaders may lead luxurious and expensive lives in full view of their constituents. Latin Americans expect their leaders to live and to behave in a manner befitting upper-class gentlemen; it is traditional that the retainer will benefit indirectly from the success of the leader. In cities and in modern towns, the employee-employer relationship is now a commercial one and political leadership is generally based upon public policy and record in office, but it is still the daring, shrewd, and adventurous politican (frequently of doubtful honesty) who catches the imagination.

One must also understand the system of social ranking of any local community as it relates to the social system of the region or the nation. The whole range of Latin American social classes will never be present in any one community. Each will contain but a segment of the various social strata present in the nation. Peasant communities, for example, consist mainly of subsistence farmers, members of an inferior social class of the nation. But peasant communities also generally have a small group of local commercial men and of government employees who are locally considered "upper class." These people of the local upper class generally lack, however, the wealth, the education, and the family connections to be recognized as "upper class" beyond the confines of their community. The landed gentry and the wealthy urbanites look down on them as slightly more fortunate peasants. Both peasant and colonos consider themselves superior to the Spanish-Indian; commercial groups, artisans, and government employees in modern towns feel that they rank higher than the generally illiterate peasant and colono; and the growing middle class in cities outrank the inhabitants of small towns. But everywhere in Latin America, despite these gradations, the essential division in the social hierarchy is between the dominating upper class and "the people."

WHAT ARE YOUR FAMILY NAMES?

One of the striking contrasts between Latin American society and our own lies in the importance assigned to kinship. In our society we tend to think of a family as consisting of a man and his wife and their children; other relatives are marginal and are often thought to impinge upon the privacy of the primary group. In Latin America, the conjugal pair and their offspring have the same important functions as they have in our society, but this nuclear unit has closer ties with a more widely extended group of kin than does ours. When a Latin American speaks of "family," he usually means an enormous group of relatives including aunts, uncles, grandparents, cousins, nephews, nieces, and in-laws.° The term "cousins" may be used for those in the second and third degree; the cousins of one's parents may be called "aunt" or "uncle."

In Latin America until recently people did not move about as frequently as North Americans. There was no moving frontier there. They did not transfer their residence from one city to another as North Americans are apt to do so easily. Thus Latin Americans have a larger number of relatives in their own community than we usually do. It is not unusual for an individual to count a hundred kinsmen in various degrees of relationship to him within his own community. A member of a well-known family may have literally hundreds of relatives. Furthermore, these large "families" maintain close ties, and there is an obligation of mutual aid among such relatives. Generally, an inner circle consisting of one's aunts and uncles, one's "brother cousins"—as the term *primo hermano* (Spanish) and *primo irmão* (Portuguese) for first cousin translates literally—and one's immediate family forms an inner group with more frequent contact and more devoted ties within the large family. But the larger circle of kin meets often. There are frequent family affairs such as birthdays, parties, baptisms, weddings, First Communions, graduation exercises, funerals, and masses for deceased members. In fact the social life of many Latin Americans is almost wholly confined to the family. Outsiders

° In a later paper (see Chapter VI) I adopted the term *parentela* for this kinship group in order to distinguish it from the conjugal or nuclear family. In social anthropological terms, the Latin American *parentela* is a "kindred."

without kinship connections may find that Latin American cities and towns have a restricted social life. Once one has been received into a family through an intimate friend, however, social life may become quite intense, since friends are often included in the many social events.

One must understand the family affiliations of one's friends and colleagues in Latin America if one wishes to understand the Latin American way of life. It is common for a business enterprise to be a family affair. People seek out a cousin when in need of a lawyer or physician. Men appoint their relatives to political and business positions not only because of a sentiment of family solidarity but also because they know their kinsmen's faults and capacities. They can count on a kinsman's loyalty. Knowledge of the surnames of the more important families in the region in which one lives in Latin America and of the social, political, and economic position of these families is important for the understanding of any local society.

Like other common patterns of Latin American culture, that of family organization differs according to region, according to community type, and according to social class. In Indian communities a widely extended kinship group is common; a result of the patriarchal family form imposed by the Spanish and of the persisting aboriginal patterns of kinship. In many Indian communities of Guatemala and southern Mexico for example, the male line of descent is emphasized to the near exclusion of the female line, an attitude reflecting the continuing influence of a system of aboriginal clans. Peasant and plantation workers share the ideal of large Latin American families, and in the more stable communities kinship groups are large; but in many peasant villages economic pressures cause many people to migrate in search of better conditions. Because people are poor, they lack the property and the economic interests that tend to keep kinship groups together. Kinsmen move away and lose touch with one another. The size of the family is thus smaller. Similarly, inhabitants of towns and workers in cities often do not have large families. They move away from their hometowns leaving their relatives behind as so many North Americans do. In general, then, the large Latin American family is limited to the isolated and stable peasant communities, to the landed gentry, and to the wealthier inhabitants of modern towns and cities. Urbanization and industrialization work against these large groups of kin. Crowded living conditions cause couples to live separately, whereas they once shared great houses or country mansions with relatives. People now live in apartments. Indivisible landholdings and other properties are no longer held by the family.

Yet in Latin American cities many large, important families are still intact. Telephones buzz between the various family households which are often found in the same district of the city. Relatives even take apartments in the same building. Then too, there are always the numerous family gatherings. The Latin American family is nowadays more fragmented than in the past, but kinship affiliations are still a highly important aspect of Latin American society.

ALMOST LIKE A KINSMAN

Consistent with the emphasis on kinship affiliations is the importance given in Latin America to ceremonial kinship ties established through the mechanism of god-parenthood (*compadrazgo* in Spanish and *compadresco* in Portuguese). This old pattern of Roman Catholic baptismal sponsorship sets up a pseudokinship relationship and a strong personal tie not only between the child and its sponsors at baptism but also between godparents and parents. Traditionally, a child may expect favors and protection from its godparents; between the god-parents and the parents there is a strong relationship of mutual aid and respect. One may borrow money from a *compadre*.* It is popularly believed that it is incest to marry a *comadre*.

In Latin America these strong compadrazgo relationships are also formed on occasions other than baptism, some of which are not directly related to Catholicism. There are god-parents of Confirmation and marriage. In northern Brazil, for example, there is the "compadre of the fire" formed by a mu-tual vow on St. John's or St. Peter's Eve. In Peru, there are padrinos of the first hair cutting of a male child, a survival of an aboriginal rite. It is not unusual in Latin America for an individual to be bound to more than twenty people by ceremonial kinship, and an important man may have hundreds of godchildren, co-fathers, and co-mothers.

In large cities and in some modern towns, the compadrazgo system may function as a mere formality, an old tradition to which lip service is offered but without the firm ties which the relationship implies. In upper-class families there is a tendency to invite relatives to serve as ritual sponsors of children, thus strengthening an existing kinship tie (rich Uncle Juan then becomes both godfather and Uncle to little Carlitos). Colonos on plantations and peasants often invite upper-class sponsors to serve as godparents to their children, in this way hoping to get favors for themselves and for the child. But it is in Spanish-Indian and peasant communities that the system persists in its most traditional form. These people establish such relation-

* *Compadre*, literally co-father, and *comadre*, literally co-mother, are the terms used between the godparents and the parents of the child. These terms are the same in Spanish and Portuguese. The godparents call their godchild *ahijado* (male) and *ahijada* (female) in Spanish; *afilhado* (male) and *afilhada* (female) in Portuguese. The godparents are called *padrino* (godfather) and *madrina* (godmother) in Spanish and *padrinho* (godfather) and *madrinha* (godmother) in Portuguese.

ships with good friends and relatives, people who are usually of approximately the same social status as themselves. The relationship is respected and taken seriously. It is felt to be "stronger than blood kinship."

Nevertheless, weak or strong, the compadrazgo system still functions in one way or another throughout Latin America. Even in great cities, a godfather will help his godchild if the situation makes it easy for him to do so. Even when mere lip service to the tradition remains, a feeling persists that there ought to be strong friendship between compadres and comadres. The compadrazgo system ties workers to their employers (a good way to gain favor with the boss is to name him padrino), and cements economic, political, and social relationships.

THEY ARE ALSO JOINERS

Perhaps because Latin Americans have such a widespread circle of personal relationships, they are not such fervent joiners as are North Americans. The numerous clubs, lodges, and other associations in Latin America do not flourish as they do with us. One type of fraternity, however, which has been important in Latin American society, is the religious brotherhood. In the early days, Third Orders, made up of pious laymen, established hospitals, asylums, and other public institutions. Religious brotherhoods devoted to particular Saints are found today throughout Latin America. In Spanish-Indian communities in Guatemala, all male citizens automatically join *cofradias* (brotherhoods) which are responsible for cooperative community tasks such as caring for the village church and repairing public buildings. In peasant villages of Brazil, *irmandades* (brotherhoods) exist with both male and female members. These brotherhoods not only organize their Saint's annual festival but also, with their formal organization and officers, are important units of community cooperation. In modern towns and cities, only the more devout Catholics belong to brotherhoods. Many Latin American urbanites feel that religious brotherhoods are old-fashioned, and they prefer to join social clubs. (The Rotary Club is strongly represented.) Yet religious associations own cemeteries, hospitals, lands, and other property, and are still important even in large cities. Official church opinion is not always in favor of brotherhoods. They sometimes grow too strong, challenging the decisions of the hierarchy and competing with the Church herself for the members' loyalty.

Except for these religious brotherhoods, associations are relatively weak compared to those in the United States. Labor unions have been formed in many countries. In some localities such as Mexico and the Caribbean area, labor unions are strong enough to have considerable political power. Elsewhere labor unions are more often creatures of the government than spontaneous organizations of working men. Political parties throughout Latin America are numerous when political conditions allow them freedom of action, for Latin Americans are fervent about their politics. But these political parties, with several noteworthy exceptions such as the Peruvian Aprista Party, the Party of the Mexican Revolution, and more recently the Christian Democratic Parties, are apt to be short lived. Most political parties change their policies almost at will, and a Latin American's loyalty to his political party, although heated and enthusiastic, tends to be a fragile one. Until very recently the large Spanish-Indian population in Indo-America was almost entirely unconscious of political groups; the peasants blindly followed their local political leaders or they too ignored politics. The colonos on plantations voted with the adminstrator or their landowning employers. Even today the majority of modern town and city people follow the lead of the dominating upper class. Few associations beyond the family have ever claimed the loyalty of Latin Americans, and political parties are, in many areas, still dominated by powerful families.

A COMMUNITY DIVIDED

Similarly Latin American community spirit may be said to be generally weak despite some very important exceptions to the contrary. One of the first acts of the Spanish conquistadors was to establish the strong Old-World *cabildo* (municipal corporation) in America. In Spanish-Indian communities a form of medieval-Spanish, municipal-administrative organization was installed by the missionaries and by civil authorities. Today many Spanish-Indian communities maintain their own local officials: the *alcalde*, or mayor; the *regidores*, or aldermen; the *mayordomos*, or clerks, and other officials. They have a strong sentiment for local government. In other types of Latin American communities, however, local government has often been smothered by regional and national interests. Plantation workers are dominated politically by their employers. In peasant communities strong localism combined with suspicion of other communities is common, but the local government is generally weak. Only a minority of the people in modern towns and cities participate fully in political life, and very few people take pride in community affairs. In some Spanish-Indian and peasant communities, spontaneous associations such as the religious brotherhoods and the esprit de corps of the community itself may offer potential bases for social action; but more commonly community spirit is weak in Latin America. Social change comes from the top, from state and federal governments, infiltrating downward to affect individual communities.

A CATHOLIC CULTURE

With the exception of a small minority, all Latin Americans are Catholics. Even the Spanish-Indians, who retain numerous aboriginal religious beliefs and who sometimes still sacrifice animals to non-Christian deities, consider themselves "very Catholic." Furthermore, even the members of fetish cults worshiping African supernaturals and performing elaborate African ritual are professed Catholics. Both African and American Indian deities are identified with Catholic saints. Spanish-Indians and members of African cults participate fully in Catholic ritual and belief. In the Amazon region medicine men using aboriginal methods practice in peasant communities and in the working class districts of large cities. In many areas—in Puerto Rico and Brazil, for example—spiritualism has taken a strong hold among the industrial laborers. Nevertheless the followers of the Indian medicine men and Spiritualists are also Catholics, conceiving these beliefs within the fabric of traditional Latin American Catholicism. Only a few *Creyentes* (Spanish) or *Crentes* (Portuguese), literally "believers"—as Protestants of all cults are often called—have broken with Catholicism. Protestants, widely known in Latin America for their religious and moral fervor, are the only major group to break the religious homogeneity of the Latin American community. The anti-Protestant outbreaks which have occurred from time to time are the only signs of religious strife in Latin America. The anti-Clericalism which has been the cause of bitter disagreements in many countries is not anti-Catholic. Instead it has been a movement opposing the political, economic, and other secular influences of the Clergy and the Church. The most aggressive anti-Cleric may often be a devout Catholic. Religious homogeneity has influenced Latin

America in many ways. It has created a bond of solidarity between peoples of widely divergent social classes and of a variety of racial groups. In many ways Latin America might be said to have a Catholic culture.

Latin American Catholicism, deriving from Spain and Portugal, takes a form similar to that known in southern Europe. It differs in many traits from that of northern Europe and the United States. Roman Catholicism has universal uniformities in ritual and theology, but Latin Americans place their own emphasis on certain orthodox concepts and forms. The saints are the central powers of Latin American Catholicism. Each community has its patron saint whose name is sometimes given to a locality or added to the name of the town or city (for example, San Juan Atitán in Guatemala and San Juan in Puerto Rico). There are miraculous saints such as the Virgin of Guadalupe in Mexico and Nosso Senhor do Bonfim in Bahia (Brazil) to whose shrines thousands of people come each year. Furthermore, many families have a saint of special devotion whom they honor as a family custom. In addition there are saints that are protectors of certain occupations or guardians of specialized groups and others with special attributes and powers. In Brazil Saint Benedict is the special protector of the Negro. Everywhere Saint Christopher, the traveler, protects taxi drivers. Saint Anthony is appealed to by women wanting husbands.

People pray to the saints, to the Virgin, and Christ for health, good crops, and protection against danger. They do likewise in all the other unpredictable crises of human life. The calendar of any Latin American community is marked by its yearly festivities on its Saints' days, which are often more important than secular national holidays. On the day of the patron saint of a community or on the festival day of a famous miracle-working saint of a region, communities are swollen by visitors who come not only out of devotion but also for the recreational activities which are part of such festivities. There is dancing, drinking, and gambling; stands with sweets and delicacies are set up. There are pageant-like processions with their inevitable rockets and fireworks. One of the most useful books for anyone working and living in Latin America is a common Roman Catholic prayer book containing not only the Mass and other ritual, but also a calendar of Saints days.

Like other aspects of Latin American culture, religious life varies according to the region and according to the type of community in which it is found. As indicated above, African elements are fused with formal Catholicism in Afro-America; in Indo-America, American Indian patterns are often integrated with Catholicism, especially in Spanish-Indian communities. For most Spanish-Indians and for many peasants religion is a community affair. Both men and women have their religious obligations to perform as members of religious associations and as members of the community. Each may address his own prayers to the protective saints of the community or to special saints of familial devotion, but in addition to private worship, public religious activities are of great importance. The saints are conceived as local powers—the St. John of one community is not the St. John named in another. The people treat their saints as powers charged with protecting them and their community. Saints not bestowing grace on the community, or not fulfilling their obligations, are known to have been whipped or hung head down in a well until they grant their benevolence. In the absence of official priests, religious ritual and activities are directed by laymen performing public obligations. In colono communities on plantations religious life, like other aspects of social life, is usually dominated by the presence of upper-class owners or administrators. The owner of a plantation may offer a festival for the workers on the day of the patron saint of the plantation, generally the special devotion of the owner rather than that of the workers. In the more mixed and complex modern towns and in cities religious life is more orthodox and more closely supervised by the clergy. There the clergy has great influence over women and children (though men tend to be only nominally Catholic), and the sacraments and laws of the Church are more carefully followed. In such places religious festivals lose many of the recreational aspects and are not generally functions of the whole community but instead become celebrations held by special groups.

Whether in peasant villages or in large metropolitan centers, however, Latin American Catholicism tends to be more mystical, more understanding of the lesser vices of men, and less strict in carrying out the principles of the orthodox Church to the letter. It is softer and more emotional than Catholicism in northern Europe and in the United States. Catholicism is part of one's life; numerous Latin Americans have not confessed, received Communion, or been to Mass in years; yet they are "traditional Catholics," and this religion touches many aspects of their lives.

A FOLK VIEW OF THE WORLD

Related to religion is the world view of a majority of Latin Americans. Throughout Latin America most people hold a basically magical and supernatural concept of the cause of phenomena and events. Although there are fine laboratories, great universities, modern hospitals, highly trained technicians and clinicians—in short, the best of modern science—in the great cities of Latin America, the majority of the people in these countries have a "folk" concept of disease and its treatment. These "superstitions," as they are called by highly educated or professionally trained Latin Americans, have been for centuries the only arms most Latin Americans have had with which to fight disease. A large proportion of all Latin Americans are illiterate° and the influence of scientific knowledge on folk belief is limited to a minority.

Folk beliefs vary considerably from one region to another. Many of them are of African or American Indian origin, but others deriving from southern Europe are widespread, even universal, throughout Latin America. The concept of the "evil eye," a belief in the power of certain individuals to inflict disease or bad luck with a mere look, is found throughout Latin America in communities of Spanish-Indians, of peasants and colonos, and even among the uneducated inhabitants of cities and modern towns. Almost universal through Latin America is the belief in "hot" (bad) and "cold" (good) foods (in Brazil the phrasing "strong" and "weak" is common), the terms indicating qualities which must be considered in diet. Similarly a belief that fright and "aires" (air or wind) cause disease, and a belief in werewolves (which appears in many local variations), are almost universal. Furthermore, medieval European folk medicine with its endless herbal remedies took root in the New World, and native plants were soon discovered to have real or imaginary medicinal properties. A belief in witchcraft as the cause of disease, which was common to all three Latin American cultural heritages, prevails today and is widespread in several forms. The belief in the power of the saints to heal illness and to send it as punishment to sinners which derives from Europe has its counterpart in African and aboriginal Indian supernatural lore, in which spirit beings were believed both to cause and to cure disease. People go to their saints asking for cures, making "*promessas*" (a vow which

° While Argentina can boast a literacy rate of almost 90%, Brazil has only about a 49% literacy. Other figures for 1950 are: Dominican Republic, 43%; El Salvador, 40%; Mexico, 54%; Venezuela, 51%; and Panama, 72%.

must be carried out in return for the saints' benevolence) and offering *ex votos,* the symbolic offerings to the saints which are so commonly found in Latin American churches.

Throughout Latin America there are also individuals who administer folk medicine, who are believed to have special religious powers and knowledge, and who are often believed to predict the future. In Spanish-Indian communities and in Amazon peasant communities, there are medicine men who cure by old American Indian techniques of sucking out the extraneous object (a beetle or a piece of bone perhaps), which is thought to have been causing illness. In Guatemala these men also tell the future by casting beans; in Amazonia they make predictions by contacting a familiar divine spirit and by numerous other methods. In Afro-America, the leaders of the fetish cults (the *pae* or *mãe de santo* of Brazil and the *papaloi* and *mamaloi* of Haitian cults) direct ritual which is often aimed at curing or protecting the people from disease. Among peasants and plantation workers there are *curanderos* (Spanish) or *curandeiros* (Portuguese)—literally curers—and *benzedores* (Portuguese, blessers) who cure by means of incantation-like traditional prayers and herbal remedies. Everywhere in small communities midwives combine their traditional methods of assisting at birth with prayer and incantation. The presence of numerous spiritualist mediums and healers in Latin American towns and cities indicates that many dwellers of these communities also have a folk rather than a scientific concept of disease.

The scope of this body of folk belief is by no means limited to disease. There are countless folk beliefs relating to almost all aspects of human affairs. The Guatemalan Spanish-Indian farmer believes that his numerous prayers and ritual are as important to the growth of his corn as the planting, the weeding, and selection of seeds. The Amazon peasant believes that he may catch *panema* (bad luck and a general incapacity at hunting or fishing) when a pregnant woman eats of his fish or game. Furthermore, even in urban literate society, Latin Americans (like North Americans who avoid the number "13" and are careful not to walk under a ladder) retain many folk beliefs even though they no longer admit them. It is bad luck to start a trip on Tuesday in Puerto Rico, for example. Throwing one's hat on a bed brings bad luck of all sorts. As in the United States, many people pay lip service to science but fear to act counter to traditional belief and practices. A mother will listen to the physician's explanation that her infant son has acquired intestinal worms and profess to believe him, but she will privately refuse to give the child fresh orange juice (it is "strong" or "hot"), because she believes that the child became ill from "fright."

These traditional folk beliefs so prevalent in Latin America often conflict with, and act as barriers to the introduction of scientific knowledge. The strict diets and the rigid *resguardo* (rules of care) which are part of the traditional means of treating any illness, for example, clash with the diets and the instructions given by physicians. The local practitioners, such as the medicine men and cult leaders, diviners, and midwives may often work against modern innovations unless their cooperation is sought.

THE ROLES OF MALE AND FEMALE

In Latin America, as in any complex civilization, the behavior of individuals varies considerably from one segment of the population to another. There is a great difference between a polished Peruvian gentleman from Lima and a Quechua-speaking Indian from the Andean highlands, and between the urbane *Carioca* of Rio de Janeiro and the *caboclo* of Mato Grosso or Amazonia. Yet throughout Latin America, certain attitudes, values, and ideals seem to be shared by the great majority of the people, and there are patterns of individual behavior—ways of acting in any given. situation—which are considered "normal" by any Latin American. These behavior patterns are not fulfilled equally by the people of all classes and communities in Latin America. They are sometimes considered antiquated by the more cosmopolitan city dwellers and by the growing middle class. Many of the behavior patterns come from the upper class, which inherited them from the landed gentry, and thus represent impossible aspirations for the poor urban dweller, the plantation worker, the colono, and the peasant. Yet they are "ideals" for these simple folk—what they would want to do, if they were able. Although the Indians also share many of these traditional Latin American behavior patterns, their own values and ideals often run counter to them; the people of Spanish-Indian communities may be expected to react differently in the same circumstances, or to fulfill the Latin American ideal superficially.

Some of the most striking ideal patterns of behavior common to most of Latin America are those relating to the roles assigned to men and women. Theoretically at least, Latin American society is male dominated. The relationship between the sexes is what might be termed the "double standard." Early in childhood the treatment of boys differs from that of girls. Most people profess a desire for male children. A father wants a son to carry on his name and the mother wants a son to please her husband. As soon as they are able to toddle, boys are expected to be mischievous, aggressive, and daring; girls are expected to be calm, obedient, and demure. These sex differences in early childhood, not unlike those of the United States, are given considerable emphasis by Latin Americans. They are anxious for their sons to show signs of being *macho* (literally, "male," although the term is generally used for a virile male animal), and for their daughters to show signs of femininity. They do not understand how North American mothers can dress their children of either sex in playsuits, blue jeans, and other asexual uniforms. Girls should be dressed in soft fluffy garments, and boys in replicas of their father's clothes.

The sexes are mixed nowadays in most Latin American primary schools, but almost everyone feels that boys and girls should be separated by the time they reach twelve or thirteen years of age. Thus most secondary schools are for one sex only. At adolescence the boy is given considerable freedom. Soon afterwards he is expected to be sexually active and to frequent "bawdy" houses. He is potential danger to any female servant and even to girls of "good family." Mothers try to ignore their sons' sexual exploits, but they may be secretly proud of this masculine behavior; fathers are often openly indulgent. After adolescence, girls should be subjected to strong controls. Parents feel certain that all young men have dishonorable designs on their daughters, and they are equally certain that no girl would be able to resist the advances of a man should she find herself alone with him. Young women should therefore be carefully guarded. They should not attend dances unless accompanied by an adult member of the family. They should not go about in the town, village, or even the neighborhood alone, but only in groups. A young man who calls at the home of a young lady several times without a good excuse excites the interest of the family. A few more calls and he may be expected to declare his intentions—to formally ask for the girl in marriage and to announce their engagement. A girl's virginity should never be doubted before her marriage; but it is absurd to think of a man being virginal on the day of his marriage. In

Brazilian rural communities men have returned brides to their fathers because they have discovered on the wedding night that "she was a ruined woman."

So many curbs on the freedom of young women added to familial suspicions of the motives of all suitors make the process of courting quite difficult. In the past, especially in wealthy families, cousins frequently married. These cousin marriages were often arranged to keep property within the family, but many of them must also have resulted from the difficulty of social relations between young people who were not of the same large family. Needless to say, young women are irritated with these restrictions. They are said to look forward to marriage as the only way of obtaining a minimum of personal freedom. Thus they look forward to early marriage at seventeen or eighteen years of age. Men, however, are not so anxious for marriage. It is illogical to think that a young man in Latin America would seek marriage simply for sexual satisfaction. On the contrary, marriage requires that he "settle down," putting an end, at least temporarily, to his amorous affairs. It is therefore thought that young men must be urged, even tricked, into marriage. Often when men are hesitant to "set the date," young women, eager for marriage, are forced to meet with their suitors secretly because the family refuses to allow a young lady to accept a suitor's visits unless the two announce their engagement. In such circumstances, people normally expect a sexual affair to result. If this takes place, the young suitor as often as not will refuse to marry the girl unless forced to do so by law or by threats. His logic is brutal: "If she offered herself to me without marriage, then she may do so to others after our marriage." Traditionally, Latin American girls who have been so seduced are expected to end up in houses of prostitution, or to live in common law marriage with her suitor until he abandons her or sees fit to "officialize the situation" with legal or religious rites. Latin American parents sigh with relief when their daughters are safely married, no matter what their opinion of the husbands.

After marriage the "double standard" continues. Absolute fidelity is expected of the wife and occasional adultery is considered normal for the husband. Unmarried girls and married women, believing that the male is unfaithful by nature, ask only that their husbands or lovers be discreet in their amorous ventures so as not to disgrace the family. Many men of high political position have been known to keep mistresses without any adverse effect on their public prestige. A divorce seems to be a greater disadvantage to a man in public life in the United States than are publicly-known infidelities in Latin America.

In keeping with the ideal of sexual bravado of the male, Latin American men fear finding themselves in the position of the wronged husband. A cuckold is considered ridiculous in all western cultures, but he is doubly so in Latin America. A man's whole position as a male is challenged. Women are expected to be weak and, from introspection and from what other men say, a husband expects men to be constantly on the hunt for sexual affairs. A cuckold has not been able to dominate his own household. He is expected to prove his masculinity by killing his wife, her lover, or both. A man's fear of becoming a cuckold and a wife's knowledge that her husband will be unfaithful given the slightest opportunity, lies at the basis of the so-called Latin jealousy.

Such behavior is considered out of date by Latin American moderns. In late years daughters of good families have taken jobs in business or in government and have even entered the professions. Almost as many women as men are enrolled in art and science courses in many Latin American universities. Young ladies nowadays have dates, with less freedom perhaps than their North American contemporaries, but still without the close chaperonage prescribed by the traditional patterns. The *paseo* (the afternoon promendes during which boys and girls circulate around the plaza or up and down an avenida so that they meet and pass by) has always provided an opportunity for brief encounters among young people. But today attendance at the movies and modern sports offers possibilities for more frequent social relations between young people. In lower economic groups girls are forced to take employment in factories and in commerce. Although peasants and plantation workers share the elite-oriented ideals of male and female behavior, it is doubtful whether they have ever been able to live up to them. Their daughters have had to help in household tasks and even in the fields. In fact, peasant women are often the main breadwinners for their families. To a large extent, therefore, the behavior patterns and values described above are maintained today only by the more "traditional" families, and are found in greater force in the provinces.

Yet these old Latin American patterns are still important in governing behavior, even of those who no longer believe in them. Parents who allow their daughters to have unchaperoned "dates" feel uncomfortable; they may be criticized by their relatives and neighbors. Even the most cosmopolitan Latin American professional man will insist on female chastity before marriage. The chaste male as an ideal type likewise does not exist. There is still considerable resistance throughout Latin America to the participation of women in public life, in business, and in the professions.

An example of the form this resistance takes is the nursing profession. Until very recently, it was difficult (and it still is in many localities) for most Latin Americans, including physicians, to understand how a woman might undertake the duties expected of a nurse and remain a "decent" woman. It was therefore not easy to attract young women into nursing. The attitude of the public and of the physicians toward nurses was that shown to a superior domestic servant. Only in recent years have strict screening of candidates and high standards for nursing schools—as well as education of the public about the role and position of the nurse—given the profession an acceptable status in Latin America.

These traditional patterns still influence people's behavior in the most cosmopolitan social circles. Men have a male social life consisting of meeting in the late afternoon at clubs or in cafes and of returning home, in many cases, barely in time for a late dinner. Married women attend family social functions and meet in feminine groups. During a social evening with mixed company, the group usually splits very early into a male and female circle, as if the sexes had little in common to discuss. A separate male and female ethos is more apparent in almost all strata of Latin American society than in the United States.

GOOD MANNERS AND DIGNITY

Latin Americans differ in other ways from North Americans. In the realm of what is spoken of as "manners," Latin Americans are much like Europeans. Their manners are more formal, more courtly, and more elaborate than ours. They may be slightly offended by the rather offhand informality of many North Americans, mistaking that manner of behavior for a lack of social form. At the same time, the social manners of Latin Americans are sometimes irritating to many North Americans, who find the bowing, the kissing of a lady's hand, and the embrace with which two men greet each other artificial and affected—if not somewhat effeminate. Latin American ladies note that North American men seldom make a point of placing them on their right in a taxi or in a private automobile. North Americans do not shake hands each time they meet and take leave of a friend, and the omission of this formality may be taken as a slight. Chewing gum is both used and manufactured in Latin America, but its use is considered particularly vulgar by many people there. There are other minutiae of behavior, too numerous to list here, in which Latin Americans differ from North Americans.

Latin Americans are in general more sensitive of their "pride" and more conscious of "face" than North Americans. In the United States the technician, the executive, and the professional man often makes a point of forgetting his social position and showing that he too can perform manual labor or menial tasks. We are proud of the high-placed man who puts on his old clothes on a day off and putters about the house, or of the director who "pitches in" working with his subordinates. Latin Americans generally do not share these values; most professional men, executives, and technicians are careful not to perform tasks that they consider to be those of subordinates and therefore below their position. To do so would endanger their status and might cause them to lose face. A professor feels that he must keep a proper distance from his students for fear that intimacy would lower him in their eyes. Latin Americans find it comical and amusing when they are told that professional men in the United States help their wives with the dishes; they feel that such a task is lacking in dignity. This sensitivity to one's proper status is directly related to the strong sense of social class in Latin America and to the "gentleman complex" mentioned earlier. The work one does is an important indicator of one's social class. It also represents a strong sense of human dignity which extends throughout the various social and economic hierarchies. An official of a small town may be offended, feeling that he has not been shown the proper respect, if he is not paid an early formal visit. A secretary in an office may feel hurt if she is asked to dust (not to clean) her employer's desk—a task which many private secretaries do without thinking in the United States. A foreman on a plantation can be offended by being asked to perform a job usually done by his workman. Even a poor peasant may feel a loss of face if one appears in his home in response to an invitation to a meal without one's suitcoat. He may feel that the occasion was not considered of sufficient importance to dress as one might dress for a more important person.

This fear of offending by not treating other people with the full respect which they feel they warrant, and the fear of losing face in the eyes of one's friends and acquaintances, frequently leads to ostentation in Latin American hospitality. It also sometimes results in a lack of hospitality; people will avoid inviting acquaintances to their homes unless they are prepared to offer them the treatment considered proper for their social status. Thus a simple peasant who invites a visitor to share his simple fare may spend as much as a month's income on the purchase of luxuries for his guest. An outsider hopeful of tasting local foods in a Latin American home may find himself dining out on expensive canned goods and "American dishes" prepared in his honor. Town folk and city dwellers are often ostentatious in their hospitality. A table of "sweets" served at a birthday reception for a child may simply groan with the great variety of the foods set out both for the children and for their parents. A luncheon may include two or three courses and several desserts. Your Latin American friend may take care of the check at a restaurant or cafe when he knows that he may have to borrow money to eke out the month. One must be careful not to offend the dignity of one's Latin American friends and colleagues, and similarly one must be careful not to allow them to extend their hospitality precariously.

Latin Americans value personalized relationships over im-

personal relationships. They are accustomed to the warm relationships within their large extended families, and they extend this mode of behavior outward to include friends. Once a
Latin American has met one's family (sometimes even if he
has simply heard that they exist), he or she will always ask
about their health in letters and at every meeting. It is a way
of putting your relations, even though they may be commercial
or professional, on a personal plane. At business and official
interviews, people generally exchange pleasantries, gossip, and
speak of common friends before taking up the business at
hand. Latin Americans often go to great extremes to avoid
carrying out even run-of-the-mill negotiations on an impersonal basis. They seek out a friend, a cousin, or a compadre in
a ministry or in a large corporation. They know that a personal
approach will be more effective, and less irritating to them,
than a "cold" approach. Latin Americans like to do small
favors for their friends and relatives—to make some purchase
for them when traveling to a distant city or to facilitate official
documents by introducing a friend or compadre in the governmental bureau responsible. They also like to ask such favors.
The outsider who lives in Latin American society will soon
learn to make use of such personal relationships. He will also
find himself involved in a veritable web of requests for small
favors. It is the Latin American way of getting things done.

Another personal characteristic of Latin Americans which
may seem somewhat strange to many North Americans is their
way of thinking which we might consider "impractical," "theoretical," or "nothing but fine talk." As John Gillin has stated it,
"Ideologically this [Latin American] culture is humanistic
rather than puritanical, if such a contrast is permissible. Intel-
lectually, it is characterized by logic and dialectics rather than
empiricism and pragmatics; the word is valued more highly
than the thing; the manipulation of symbols (as in argument)

is more cultivated than the manipulation of natural forces (as in mechanics)." (Gillin 1947b: 244.)

Latin Americans are thus experts at creating logical and well-reasoned plans, but they may lose interest in the dull details of the execution. The famous professors are those with a brilliant oratorical style in the classroom. Latin American professionals and technicians are strong on theoretical aspects of their fields, but sometimes lacking in practical application. People love to argue; the violent discussions, which to an unpracticed ear might seem almost quarrels, are but the talk of friends exhibiting their dialectic abilities. Latin Americans admire brilliance and mental agility, even though they are aware that it is sometimes superficial. A recently deceased Brazilian was much admired because he "could speak brilliantly about any subject even though he might know little about it." He had been a novelist, a literary critic, a physician, a professor of public health, and an expert on education during his lifetime. Traditionally Latin American education emphasizes memory over learning by doing. Professional schools are generally strong on theory and short on practical courses. Despite their technical deficiencies in industry, in transportation, in farming, and in other fields, there are first rate scientists and professional men in almost all Latin American countries. This propensity for theory, this "impracticality," has produced men of outstanding creative ability in many fields.

Finally, Latin Americans are a warm, overt, friendly, and hospitable people. Latin Americans like others to be like themselves—warm and overt. They like people to expand, to talk, and to tell about themselves. They especially like to hear about those aspects of your life which their own culture emphasizes. They will want to know about your family, including your distant cousins. They are very pleased when foreigners carry pictures of their family as so many North Americans do. Latin Americans are proud of North American social democracy and of the Lincoln story ("from log cabin to White House"); but if you are a technician or a professional man they will presume that you were born of the upper class. They will be curious about the North American system of race relations and many will ask you to explain it! In small towns they will wonder how you can be a Protestant (if you are) and still smoke (if you do). They will welcome a description of your home town. They will marvel at the products of North American industrialism, but they hope that you will not continually draw comparisons to their disadvantage. Latin Americans will be pleased to see that you recognize some of the positive values in their way of life. When a Latin American says "My house is yours," he may not mean it literally, but he would like to.

[III]

A TYPOLOGY OF
LATIN AMERICAN SUBCULTURES

I

ONE of the most perplexing problems in the study of complex national or regional cultures such as those of Latin America is the diversity of patterns and institutions which they contain. There are a series of institutions, values, and modes of behavior which constitute throughout Latin America a "cultural common denominator" and which distinguish Latin American culture from other major culture spheres of the Western world (see Gillin 1947b and Wagley 1948). But the "common denominator" of modern Latin America does not consist simply of those institutions, values, and behavior patterns held in common by most of the Latin American population. Regular cultural differences within the complex and heterogeneous national societies must also be considered. A conceptual framework based on these differences is much needed to provide a context for the extant data and to guide future research. This is especially true with respect to the numerous anthropological community studies, whose contribution to our knowledge of a national culture is often lessened by an inadequate definition

This paper was written in collaboration with Marvin Harris, who has generously allowed it to be published in this book. It was originally published as part of a special issue on Latin America in the *American Antropologist*, Vol. 57, No. 3, June, 1955.

of just what variety of the national culture is being considered —or, in other words, what segment of the diverse population they treat. The purpose of the present article is to suggest a taxonomic system of subcultures which we hope will have operational utility throughout Latin America.

This attempt to provide a classificatory system for ordering cultural data on Latin America is obviously not unique. As we shall discuss in more detail below, Redfield (1941), by implication at least, distinguished four types of communities for Yucatán, although only the folk and urban types were emphasized. Steward (1953; 1956) and his associates in the Puerto Rican project isolated a series of significant Puerto Rican subcultures for study.* And recently a series of articles has been published dealing mainly with Latin America, aimed at refining and extending Redfield's folk-urban concepts. Most of these discussions of Redfield's classification and most attempts to develop a sociocultural taxonomic system have dealt with varieties of whole local communities treated as whole societies. This is to be expected from a discipline whose traditional research methods involved prolonged, sedentary, and intimate contact with a restricted locale and the analysis of local sociocultural wholes. But it is apparent that many of the communities studied in Latin America by anthropologists have an internal heterogeneity of culture patterns made up of class differences, differences between rural and urban residents of the same community, and other factors too numerous to list. It is therefore often difficult to classify the culture of a whole local community as "folk culture," as "urban culture"—or as "Indian," "mestizo," or "creole." The present taxonomy of subcul-

---

* Our proposed taxonomy of Latin American subculture types and our general approach to the concept of national subcultures owe much to Julian Steward and his associates in the Puerto Rican project. The relationship between several of our subculture types and those distinguished in Puerto Rico will be indicated below.

tures attempts to distinguish between culture and society and to take into account not only the differences among communities but also internal cultural heterogeneity within communities.

We distinguish nine significant Latin American subculture types. They are called "subcultures" because they are variations of a larger cultural tradition and represent the way of life of significant segments of the Latin American population. They are called "types" because their content differs according to the environment, history, and distinctive local traditions of the nation or subregion in which they are found. Thus the subculture types we have called "Peasant" differ in content in the western countries of Central and South America, with their strong American Indian tradition, from the same type found in the West Indies and lowland Brazil, which has felt strong African influences. Yet it seems to us that Peasant subcultures throughout Latin America share certain basic features which make it possible to include them in the same typological category.

At least in a preliminary fashion, the following subculture types would seem to be useful for ordering the universe of Latin American cultural materials: (1) *Tribal Indian*, comprising the cultures of the few remaining aboriginal peoples; (2) *Modern Indian*, resulting from the fusion of aboriginal and, in the main, Iberian institutions and culture patterns of the sixteenth and seventeenth centuries; (3) *Peasant*, carried by the relatively isolated horticultural peoples of Latin America (and frequently by the lower classes of small isolated towns), who are called variously *mestizos, cholos, ladinos, caboclos,* or other local terms; (4)*Engenho Plantation*, the subculture of the workers on family-owned estates; (5) *Usina Plantation*, the way of life on the large, modern, corporation-owned agricultural establishments; (6) *Town*, the way of life of inhabitants of the middle and upper classes in the numerous settlements serving as administrative, market, and religious centers throughout Latin America; (7) *Metropolitan Upper Class,* characteristic of the highest socioeconomic strata in the large cities and of the owners of plantations; (8) *Metropolitan Middle Class,* characteristic of an emerging group of big-city professional and white-collar workers and owners of medium-sized businesses; and (9) *Urban Proletariat,* characteristic of a mass of unskilled and semiskilled industrial and menial workers in the larger cities.

Undoubtedly there are many other important Latin American subcultural types, and it is hoped that the present taxonomy will be refined and extended—or that it will stimulate others to formulate a more useful system.

II

TRIBAL INDIAN TYPES

In 1500 when the Europeans came to that part of the New World which is now Latin America, the natives of the lowlands (except for certain parts of the circum-Caribbean) lacked true tribal or political organization. There were innumerable "tribes" made up of villages or bands united only by a common language, common custom, and the consciousness of forming "a people" united against all outsiders. The power of chiefs seldom extended beyond one or a few villages or bands; and the tribes, sometimes even the villages or bands of the same tribe, were often at war with one another. The population was sparse in aboriginal times, and disease, slavery, and European warfare against these highly divided groups rapidly led to the decimation and extinction of the native peoples in many localities. Nowadays only an insignificant few of these tribal groups persist in localities such as the Chaco, the headwaters of the

Amazon tributaries, and on isolated reservations and mission stations. Such tribesmen constitute an insignificant segment of the modern Latin American population, and as long as they retain their aboriginal cultures and their identity as tribesmen they are, in reality, carriers of distinct cultures within the geographic boundaries of Latin America and not carriers of subcultures of modern Latin America. However, the process of acculturation now taking place among these tribal groups does pertain to the study of Latin American culture, and, as Foster pointed out in his discussion of the folk-culture concept, it is important to distinguish between tribal cultures and the mixed rural cultures of Latin America (1953:162).

MODERN INDIAN TYPES

The Indians of the highland regions of Latin America must be included in any study of modern Latin American culture. Although their way of life differs strikingly from that of the nationals of the countries in which they live, they share many patterns and institutions—mainly of European origin—with the other inhabitants, and numerically they are an important segment of the population. Unlike the lowlands, the highland region was inhabited by a dense aboriginal population organized into native states. After the initial shock of armed conquest and disease, these peoples were brought under the control of the Spanish colonials. Through mechanisms such as the *encomienda, repartimiento, mita,* and other forms of forced labor, they were made to work for their conquerors and were integrated into colonial society. Missionaries taught them Catholicism and, in many cases, they were concentrated into Spanish-type villages in which a European form of community organization was forced upon them. They borrowed freely from the European culture of the sixteenth and seventeenth centuries—a culture which in many respects contained as many folk features as their own. By the beginning of the eighteenth century, a new culture had taken form among these peoples out of the fusion of aboriginal and colonial Spanish patterns. Unchanged in its main outlines this culture persists today; it constitutes an important variant of national patterns in many highland countries.

Modern Indians generally speak an aboriginal language, although they may also be bilingual. Some of them work in mines, on coffee fincas, or on large haciendas, but most characteristically they are horticulturalists planting native American crops, although many European plants have also been adopted. Despite the tendency to individualize landholdings which began in the nineteenth century, among many Modern Indian groups the community is still the landholding unit. Community cohesion usually persists at a high level despite the encroaching power of the national states. Indian *alcaldes*, *regidores*, and other officials are often maintained alongside the national bureaucracy.

While the Modern Indian is nominally Catholic, it is characteristic that a large segment of aboriginal belief has been fused with Catholic ideology. In addition, Catholic saints are endowed with local characteristics and powers. The Indians of each community generally think of themselves as ethnic units separate from other Indian groups and from the nationals of the country in which they reside; they are the people of Santiago Chimaltenango, of Chamula, or of Chucuito, rather than Guatemalans or Peruvians. Frequently they wear a distinctive costume which identifies them as Indians of a particular pueblo, and it is characteristic for the Indians of each community to be endogamous.

Numerous examples of this subcultural type have been studied in Latin America by anthropologists. The Indians of Santiago Chimaltenango (Wagley 1941, 1950), of Chichicastenango (Bunzel 1952), of Panajachel (Tax 1953), of Quintana Roo, Yucatán (Villa 1945), of Kauri (Mishkin 1946), and of Chucuito in Peru (Tschopik 1951)—to mention but a few—are carriers of Modern-Indian-type subcultures. Yet, as noted above, few of these communities contain carriers of only the Modern Indian subculture type. In most of these communities, there are also a few non-Indians, carriers of a Peasant-type subculture, who form an integral part of community life. Any full community study must treat not only the two subcultures of these communities but also the "caste-like" relationship between them. As Gillin has written, "Each group [ladino and Indian] has culture patterns more or less exclusive to itself, but the two castes are part of a reciprocal pattern which characterizes the community as a whole" (1951:11). Too often our community studies have treated Modern Indian subcultures as if they were isolated tribal groups.

PEASANT TYPES

Throughout Latin America the people who inhabit rural farms and the numerous small, isolated agricultural villages have a way of life which is analogous in many respects to that of peasants in other part of the world. Latin American peasants physically may be American Indians, Negroes, or Europeans, or mixtures of these racial stocks. They are the people who are called mestizos (Mexico and other countries), ladinos (Guatemala), cholos (Peru), and *caboclos, tabareus, caipiras,* and *matutos* (Brazil). In some respects, their way of life is similar to that of the Modern Indian. Most often they are horticulturalists using the same "slash-and-burn" techniques of farming as the Modern Indians, and they frequently depend upon native plants such as maize, manioc, and potatoes for food.

As stated earlier, Peasant-type subcultures are strongly flavored with aboriginal traits in some areas, for example in the

Amazon Valley, where native shamanism is an intergral part of peasant religion. In other areas, such as the West Indies and the Guianas, African traits persist in varying degrees among the Peasant subcultures just as American Indian traits do elsewhere. But everywhere Peasant-type subcultures are characterized by a predominance of archaic European patterns, which survive alongside the American Indian or African patterns and which are slowly giving way to new national patterns and institutions. Unlike the Modern Indians, Peasants generally consider themselves nationals of the country in which they reside. Although they tend to be regional in their loyalties and to have but a vague idea of what it means to be a member of a nation, national patterns and institutions play a larger role in Peasant than in Modern Indian subcultures. Peasant subculture economies are closely tied in with regional and national economies. There is fairly extensive participation in commercial transactions through the medium of markets, to which Peasant farmers regularly go to sell their surplus products for cash. Peasants maintain accounts at stores and trading posts from which they receive goods of nationwide circulation such as kerosene, steel tools, cloth, thread, and sewing machines.

Peasants characteristically speak the national language (Spanish or Portuguese), although sometimes an aboriginal tongue (for example, the Tarascan of the Michoacan mestizos), or, as in Haiti, a creole, is spoken. Peasants participate to some extend in political life, voting if there are elections and if they have the franchise. Catholicism in Peasant subcultures tends to be more orthodox than that of the Modern Indian. Peasants share national fashions, values, and aspirations, although in all of these they are "behind the times" since they tend to be isolated from the centers of diffusion. Thus young men may play soccer if it is the national sport, as it is in Brazil. Peasants often celebrate national holidays and perhaps know something of their national heroes. Literacy is valued as an aid in social and economic improvement. Nowadays Peasants tend to dress after the style of the city as soon as such styles are known and people can afford them. Because such people are generally poor, illiterate, and isolated, they have little in the way of modern technological facilities such as electric lights, motor-driven vehicles, and modern housing.

Again, it is not difficult to cite examples of this type of Latin American subculture which have been studied by anthropologists. Subcultures of both the modern Indian and Peasant types tend to be carried by relatively small and simply organized social units which lend themselves to investigation by the traditional field techniques of ethnology. The rural agriculturalists living in the environs of Moche in Peru (Gillin 1947 a), those of the community of Tzintzuntzan in Mexico (Foster 1948), those of Cruz das Almas in southern Brazil (Pierson 1952), those of Itá in the Brazilian Amazon (Wagley 1953b), and those of Marbial Valley in Haiti (Métraux 1951) are carriers of subcultures which correspond to the Peasant type. The Small Farmer subculture of Puerto Rico would also seem to correspond to this category (Steward 1953; Manners 1956).

But it must be emphasized that most of the communities mentioned above also contain people who are not peasants, people who are not even rural, but rather townsmen with urban aspirations and urban patterns of behavior. The subculture of these people will be considered below as the Town type. Due to the tendency to regard "folk culture" as a way of life characteristic of a type of community, the folk subcultures (or in our terms, Peasant subcultures) of such communities have often been emphasized to the exclusion of the nonfolk elements. The restudy of Redfield's Tepoztlán by Lewis (1951) is an example of how the concept of a homogeneous folk community needs to be qualified in view of the internal heterongeneity of cultural patterns found in rural communities.

The fact probably is that the carriers of Peasant-type subcultures live everywhere in communities which also contain carriers of Town-type subcultures, whose ties with national life are the intermediate bonds by which the peasant is also tied into national life. Indeed, many peasants are actually town dwellers who have their domiciles in town and their farms in the nearby area. Although settlements inhabited exclusively by people who have a homogeneous Peasant subculture are extremely common, it is a distortion to view them as isolated communities, or even as total communities. Because the Peasant subculture is distinguished from the Modern Indian precisely on the grounds of greater identification with and participation in national patterns and institutions, it is clear that a group of peasants can only be *part* of a community, and that the terms "folk society" and "folk culture" are misleading when applied to a community which actually and necessarily contains more than one subculture. It may help to clarify the matter if the communities in which peasant households, hamlets, and villages occur are thought of as larger Town-Peasant communities, implying that Town and Peasant subcultures must be considered together if a proper understanding of either is to be attained. This symbiotic relationship between Peasant subcultures and Town subcultures ("folk and nonfolk") has been recently emphasized by Foster (1953:169 ff.).

ENGENHO PLANTATION AND USINA PLANTATION TYPES

The Europeans who settled in the Caribbean and in the lowland parts of northern South America did not find the riches in gold and silver or the large aboriginal labor force which their contemporaries encountered in the highlands. But by the middle of the sixteenth century sugar cane had become an important commercial crop in Brazil and in parts of the West

Indies. For a time the great wealth which sugar brought to this lowland region was comparable to that derived from minerals in the highlands. From the Old World the planters brought a commercialized version of large-scale agricultural enterprise, which had its roots in sixteenth-century Europe and even earlier in the ancient Mediterranean world. In the New World this agricultural system was modified by the massive use of slave labor, by the exigencies of sugar as a commercial crop, and by the physical and social environment of the New World colonies. The result was the New World plantation—the hacienda, the finca, the estancia, the fazenda, or whatever it happened to be called in the various countries.

Such plantations came to form veritable communities, or neighborhoods of larger communities, with their own variety of Latin American culture. Although large-scale agricultural establishments differ from one part of Latin America to another and in accordance with the crop to which they are dedicated (for example, sugar, coffee, bananas, cotton, cacao, henequen), there are many social and cultural similarities among them. Furthermore, some fundamental changes in the way of life on Latin American plantations have followed essentially the same developmental processes throughout the whole area, despite differences in the commercial crops.

The general characteristics of the Engenho plantation subculture type may best be illustrated by reference to plantations dedicated to sugar cane, which was for centuries Latin America's most important commercial crop. Although there were local differences, sugar-cane plantations during the period of slavery seem to have followed a similar pattern throughout the area. The center of the plantation, and of the community or neighborhood which it formed, was the mansion in which the owner, his large family, and the many domestic servants lived. A chapel which was either attached to the mansion or situated near it, served as the church for the owners and for the slave workers. Behind the mansion were the slave quarters—a street of huts. Nearby were sheds used to store tools and equipment and to house the oxen and other animals. A storehouse, where the food and other supplies for the field hands were kept and periodically distributed, was also a common feature. There was also the engenho (Spanish *ingenio*), a small sugar factory containing a mill driven by hand, by animal traction, or by water power. Such plantations were generally situated on waterways which furnished easy transportation to market centers. Characteristically, the plantation settlement pattern was a concentrated one resembling that of a small village.

The number of people on such plantations was generally not large during the slave period. On the average no more than two hundred to three hundred people lived on a relatively large sugar plantation, and within this small "village-like" society social relations tended to be intimate and highly personal. The members of the owner's family were tied together into a large, extended patriarchal group. Between these aristocrats and the slaves there was a stable set of relations often accompanied by personal intimacy and intense loyalty. It was, in other words, a "caste" society made up of Negro slaves and European owners in which each caste was conscious of the rights and obligations of the other. Leadership was provided automatically by the dominant European group, and economics, religion, and almost all aspects of life were directed and controlled by the aristocratic owner or his administrators.

The abolition of slavery, the vagaries of the international market, and finally the industrialization of sugar refining brought about important changes in the old colonial sugar plantations. However many plantations may still be found throughout Latin America which strongly resemble the old engenho despite the substitution of wage labor for slavery and other innovations. Such plantations are still owned, and often administered, by descendants of the same aristocratic slave-owning families of the nineteenth century. The workers, some of whom may actually be descendants of former slaves, show the same dependency and loyalty toward their employers as the slaves are said to have shown for their masters. Each of these engenho-type plantations, with its cluster of houses and sheds and its small chapel, forms, as in the past, a small concentrated village or neighborhood (Smith 1963:444 ff.) Economic life is still focused on monoculture, and little land or time is left for the workers to grow their own gardens. Today the sugar factory itself is no longer a part of the engenho-type plantations. The engenho-type plantations have become, instead, suppliers of sugar cane to large mechanized sugar mills, or *usinas*, which do the processing and marketing. But in many respects the way of life on these old-style plantations has changed remarkably little since the nineteenth century.

Here again the community unit consists of the carriers of two distinct subcultures, that of the workers and that of the owners. Although it would be tempting to make the engenho plantation community unit and the Engenho Plantation subculture coincide, the fact is that the plantation owner is usually also an urban Latin American cosmopolitan who is found in the upper strata of the principal large cities. Since early colonial times he has had both a "town house" and his place in the country, and has alternated his residence, sometimes seasonally, between one and the other. His employees, formerly his slaves or peons, including his domestic servants in town as well as the workers in the country, are treated by him with characteristic patriarchal, intimate, and usually benevolent concern. To this treatment the engenho plantation worker responds with loyalty and attitudes of dependence. It is this dependence and allegiance to the *patrao* (boss), together with the dis-

tinctive land tenure, occupational, and communal arrangements peculiar to the monoculture regime, which distinguish
Engenho Plantation subcultures from Peasant subcultures.*

Throughout Latin America, a transition from the engenho
plantation to the modern industrialized agricultural enterprise
has occurred or is now taking place. We have called the newer
form the usina plantation, from the term used for the modern
industrialized sugar mill.† Speaking again in terms of sugar
plantations, as steam-driven mills were introduced capital
came to play a more important role than land. The central-
power-driven usina could process and distribute far more effi-
ciently than the smaller installations, and so the small plantations came to depend more and more upon the usina to process
the cane. Gradually great corporations have bought out the
smaller properties and welded them together into large agricultural factories. There is a transitional phase, however, in
which each engenho plantation is administered as a separate
unit by employees of the corporation. During this phase much
of the old way of life continues. This period of transition is one
which is particularly vulnerable to social tension and economic
instability. The workers have lost the security provided by the
traditional patrão, and the new system of social welfare and
social security of the national government has not as yet been
extended to cover them.

Then, as industrialization progresses, it becomes more effi-
cient to fuse these smaller properties into one large, centralized

* Our *Engenho* Plantation type seems to correspond to the Coffee
Hacienda subculture of Puerto Rico (see Steward 1953: 98–100; Wolf
1956a).

† In tracing the development of a Puerto Rican sugar plantation, Mintz
has distinguished three historical periods or types of sugarcane plantations: the "slave-and-*agregado*," the "family-type *hacienda*," and the
"corporate land-and-factory combine" (1953b). The first corresponds to
our engenho plantation during slavery, the second to our engenho plantation after slavery, and the third to our usina plantation.

commercial farm. Where this process has been completed, as in Cuba, Puerto Rico, and Brazil, the result is a type of Plantation subculture which differs profoundly from that of the old-style engenho plantation. The traditional pattern of intimacy and mutual dependence between the workers and their employers is replaced by a more strictly economic relationship between the workers and the administrators and officials of the corporation. The local group becomes larger as the number of workers increases, and the social unit is more heterogeneous as new specialized occupations appear. The workers, without the old emotional ties to their fellows and to their employers, are more mobile than before, often leaving the plantation to seek higher wages elsewhere. The usina plantation is more closely integrated with national institutions and culture patterns. Labor unions are sometimes active among the workers, and social welfare legislation is enforced more often than in the engenho plantation. There may be electric lights, modern housing, schools, medical clinics, public health facilities, and excellent communications with the metropolitan centers. The workers on such establishments seem to have a way of life more similar to that of the growing urban-industrial proletariat of Latin America than to that of the workers on the engenho plantations. Mintz has characterized the workers on these large commercial plantations as the "Rural Proletariat" (1953a: 139 ff.; 1956).

The discussion of these two types of Plantation subcultures has been based on plantations involved in sugar production. Of course, large-scale agricultural estates that grow other kinds of commercial crops for export are also found in Latin America. Such crops as cacao, coffee, maté tea, henequen, and cotton are also produced on large-scale, monoculture plantations. It is probable that the regime of exploitation of each different crop determines distinctive sociocultural conditions. Thus when more data become available it may be convenient to formulate a series of additional subtypes for Engenho and Usina Plantation subcultures based on crop specialties. Livestock ranches, for example, with their small number of workers, their exclusion of female laborers, and their saturation with a kind of horse complex, clearly merit treatment as a subtype.

From another point of view, the widespread occurrence of sharecropping suggests an additional sector of refinements for our categories. Sharecropping of a commercial crop as a substitute for wages can probably be subsumed under the category of Engenho Plantation subcultures. Relationships between the owner and his workers approach the highly personal ones characteristic of engenho plantations, with the employer offering assistance in a crisis and in many instances being the sole purchaser of his tenants' produce. The individual sharecropping regime, however, may act to reduce the community cohesion characteristic of nucleated wage laborers on other engenho-type plantations.

For the purpose of this paper, it seems sufficient to set forth the hypothesis that at least two broad types, the Engenho Plantation and the Usina Plantation subcultures, may be found throughout Latin America. No matter what crop the plantation produces, there has been a transition from the old traditional enterprise to the modern industrialized establishment analogous to that which has taken place in sugar production. Everywhere this transition has involved a shift from a more personal and stable set of relations between the classes to a mobile, impersonal one based on economic values and urban standards. It has involved a change from a small and relatively homogeneous society to a larger and more variegated one; and it has led to a more important role for national institutions and patterns on all levels of plantation life.

It is surprising that so few examples of the Plantation sub-cultures of either type have been studied by anthropologists, especially in view of the obvious numerical importance of plantation workers in the Latin American population and in view of the importance of plantation production in the national economies of the Latin American nations. A study of an Engenho Plantation subculture has been carried out by Hutchinson as part of a community study in the Recôncavo region of Bahia in Brazil (1957). A study of a government-owned sugar plantation was made by Elena Padilla Seda in Puerto Rico (1956), and on the same island Mintz studied a large sugar plantation owned and operated by a commercial corporation (1956). Loomis and Powell have studied a Costa Rica finca producing sugar and coffee, and have given us a comparison of a hacienda and a peasant community in rural Costa Rica (1951). A study of a community in Brazil in which there are cacao-producing plantations has been carried out by Anthony Leeds (1957). If the present classification of Latin American subculture types serves no other purpose, it indicates that a large segment of the Latin American population—and an important variant of the culture of the area—has been relatively neglected in our field investigations.

TOWN TYPES

Towns where periodic fairs are held and which serve as the administrative and religious centers for rural districts are old in Latin America. They have their roots both in the European and in the aboriginal traditions. With the improvement of transportation (especially with the use of trucks), many of these towns have become regional markets similar to the market towns that serve the rural United States. As these market centers enlarge their range of trading, the rural population no longer produces only for local consumption but begins to plant by more modern methods cash crops that are sold on the national market. The towns thus become more closely integrated with national economic and political life. Their populations increase, and new concepts and patterns are introduced from the cities. Life in these larger towns is more like that of the great urban centers, by which they are more directly influenced, than like that of the surrounding countryside.

Yet in Latin America today there are still innumerable small towns serving only an immediate rural area and preserving many traditional patterns. Such towns cannot be understood without reference to the whole communities of which they are the centers. For it is characteristic of Town subcultures that their "city folk" look down upon the "country people" as "hicks," and that behavior patterns, values, standards of dress, speech, and etiquette differ for the upper-class townspeople as opposed to both the lower-class townspeople and to the inhabitants of the rural countryside.

As we have already indicated, such towns are part of communities which include two strongly contrasting subcultures. The contrast between the two corresponds to a marked schism in socioeconomic class status between a non-farming, landlord, business-owning, bureaucratic, "white-collar" group and a farming, manual-laboring group. Within the town itself, there are a small number of people who are craft specialists, such as shoemakers, blacksmiths, and carpenters, who are permanent residents of the town, and who do not engage in agricultural activities. From the point of view of the local upper class these people may be "hicks" just as much as the town-dwelling and country-dwelling farmers. Although these artisans themselves often regard the rural people with condescension, they are generally more closely related (by kinship, by marriage, by social and cultural values, by economics, and by social intercourse) to the rural farmers than to the town upper class. The stigma of poverty, of illiteracy, and of manual labor is on both groups. Thus in isolated areas, town-dwelling farmers, town-dwelling artisans and laborers, and domestic servants can usually be classed as carriers of a Peasant subculture. But such people represent a gradient of contact between isolated semi-subsistence farmers and the upper-class townspeople who are carriers of Town subculture.

The life of the upper-class townsman differs radically from that of the carriers of the Peasant subcultures. The small-town upper-class "urbanite" manifests in many respects an archaic version of the ideals and patterns of the big-city cosmopolitans and the plantation gentry of bygone days. Although upper-class townspeople are often more familiar with the geography of the nearest large city than with the geography of the rural areas of the community they live in, and although they seek to emulate cosmopolitanism with respect to dress, manners, and outlook, they are often thwarted in these ambitions by the incompleteness and inaccuracy of their notions of the contemporary standards of sophistication. Thus, in most Latin American small towns, culture patterns persist which are today considered old-fashioned in the cities. Courting, for example, is closely chaperoned, and it is a common sight to see a young man quietly conversing with his fiancée from the street while she looks down at him safely from the window of the house. And in the plaza there is often the *paseo*, during which the young men circulate in one direction as the young ladies go in the other.

Except in regions where there are large plantations owned by a rural gentry, upper-class townsmen control most of the political and economic power in the community. Their political life is intense, and there is great competition for the support of lower-class peasant electors. Upper-class social life frequently revolves around clubs which sponsor dances and other forms of entertainment from which the peasants are excluded. Upper-class Catholicism is more orthodox in Town subcultures than in Modern Indian and Peasant subcultures. More emphasis is placed on church-going and on formal sacraments, less on household saints and unorthodox cults. Where deviations from Catholic tradition occur, they are apt to take the form of Prot-estantism or spiritualism. Upper-class townsmen have radios, receive mail, magazines, and newspapers, and send their children to be educated in big-city high schools and colleges. They own fashionable clothing and often have servants to cook, wash, carry water, and take care of their house for them.

The existence of Town subcultures in isolated communities furnishes the key to the problem of the relationship of Peasant subcultures to lines of national political and economic subcultures to lines of national political and economic integration. Local standards are set and maintained by this sociocultural segment, and it is through the upper class of the town that changes emanating from national legislation and metropolitan influences must filter before reaching the peasant stratum (see Foster 1953:169 ff.).

Many studies of local variations of Town subcultures have been made in Latin America by anthropologists as part of the study of communities which also include Peasant or even Modern Indian subcultures. But frequently in such studies it is difficult to know which data pertain to the Town subculture and which to the subculture of the community's rural population. The town of Cunha in São Paulo, Brazil (Willems 1947), and the town of Moche in Peru (Gillin 1947a)—a part from the rural peasants of both communities—seem to have subcul-tures of this type. Two community studies recently carried out in Brazil—Monte Serrat in the arid northeast (Zimmerman 1952) and Minas Velhas in the central mountain region (Harris 1956)—distinguish between the Town and Peasant subcultures. In general, however, anthropologists have tended to emphasize the Latin American Peasants or Modern Indians. A large portion of the population in countries such as Argentina, Uruguay, Paraguay, Brazil, Chile, and Colombia live in small towns. Not until we know more about the way of life distinctive of these small urban centers will our knowledge of Latin American culture be anything more than relatively superficial. It is not, in our opinion, the so-called mestizo or creole patterns (in our terms, Peasant subcultures) which, as Gillin maintains (1947b), are the emergent culture patterns of Latin America. Rather, the predominant trend in contemporary Latin America would seem to be toward Town subcultures which are closely identified with the urbanized and industrialized world.

METROPOLITAN UPPER CLASS, METROPOLITAN MIDDLE CLASS, AND URBAN PROLETARIAT TYPES

Little research has been carried out, either by sociologists or by anthropologists, on the modern Latin American city. As far as anthropology is concerned, such cities pose a difficult problem in research methodology because the traditional field methods are best applied to relatively small populations and relatively homogeneous societies. The problem of class differences in the Latin American urban centers presents one of the most pressing and difficult challenges to students of Latin American culture. There is a critical lack of information about socioeconomic stratification as well as about the basic subcultural differences which attend the various levels. Accordingly in this paper we can do little more than speculate about the subcultures to be found in the great metropolitan centers of Latin America.

It is quite clear to all who have visited Latin America that although the metropolitan centers share much with cities throughout the Western World, they have their own peculiar characteristics. Caplow has pointed out two distinctive features of Latin American cities (1952:255):

> . . . those traits which are common to metropolitan cultures everywhere in the modern world are most concentrated in groups of high status, whence they are diffused rather raggedly down through the social system of each community; second, that there is more cultural variation within the Latin American city than within most cities of the United States or Europe.

These two differences between the cities of Latin America and those of the United States and Europe explain why the population of the Latin American city often seems, in a sense, to be smaller than the census data indicate. This appears to be the case because the number of people who participate effectively in city life (that is, those who buy newspapers, attend the cinema, have electric lights, telephone service, and so forth) is exceedingly small compared with the actual population. The way of life of the largest proportion of city dwellers —those who live outside the stream of city life—differs little in many respects from that of the inhabitants of rural areas. In fact a large number of these Latin American city dwellers have but recently migrated from the rural zones.

The people of the Metropolitan Upper Class attempt to maintain, as far as possible, the traditional patterns and ideals of an aristocratic landed gentry. It is this group which participates in and generally dominates local and national politics. Its members are absentee landlords, high-level government employees and officials, owners of industry and large commercial enterprises, and many well-to-do doctors, lawyers, and other professionals. Whether or not such people are the actual descendants of the landed gentry of the nineteenth century or descendants of immigrants or others who have recently achieved wealth and position, they tend to adopt many of the ideal patterns of nineteenth-century agrarian society. There is an emphasis among them on widely extended kinship ties which is strongly reminiscent of nineteenth-century aristocratic society. They have a disdain for manual labor, an admiration for courtly manners, and a love of luxury. But, at the same time, it is this group in Latin America that permits its daughters to have "dates" and allows them to enter the professions, thus breaking the old traditional patterns of highly chaperoned courtship and the confinement of women to purely domestic realms.

At least the more educated and the wealthier members of this group are in close touch with Europe and the United States. Until the last two decades they looked to France for innovations, and French tended to be their second language. Recently, however, the United States has supplanted France in this respect, and English has become the preferred foreign language. Hence the Metropolitan Upper Class tends both to preserve old traditional forms and to be the innovator in accepting new forms from abroad. The new forms are then diffused down to the lower class of the city, outward to the townspeople and ultimately to the peasants and the plantation workers. To a large extent, therefore, many of the ideal patterns common to the other Latin American subcultures derive from Metropolitan Upper Class patterns.

Anthropologists have not written studies specifically pertaining to the subculture of the Metropolitan Upper Class with the exception of Raymond Scheele, whose study was part of the Puerto Rican Project directed by Steward (1956:418–62). To date most of our information comes from data acquired by anthropologists and others during their casual relations with Latin Americans of this group and from what Latin Americans write about themselves. It is suggested that the ethnographic method should be used in the study of representative local segments of the Latin American upper class. Until this is done, much of what we say about this important segment of Latin American culture will remain hypothetical.

Even less of a concrete nature is known about the Metropolitan Middle Class and Urban Proletariat subcultures. The middle class in the large cities of Latin America is made up of a rapidly increasing group of first-generation professionals and of white-collar workers in business and government. Most observers tend to agree that this middle class maintains standards of material consumption and prestige closely patterned after those of the Metropolitan Upper Class. Its members place a high value on freedom from manual labor, and in matters of housing, clothing, and etiquette consciously strive to reduce the gap between themselves and their wealthier models. The presence in the cities of a vast substratum of marginal wage earners that is constantly replenished by rural emigration permits the Metropolitan Middle Class to employ domestic servants and to avoid the stigma of menial labor.

But there is intense competition for white-collar positions, and salaries are often insufficient to maintain leisure-class standards in other respects. One result noted by many observers has been the multiplication of the number of jobs held by each middle-class wage earner. Some high school teachers in Rio de Janeiro, for example, teach in as many as five or six different schools and have to rush from one place to the next with split-second precision in order to arrive at their classes on time. Caught between low incomes and high standards of consumption modeled after those of the upper class, the middle class if forced to devote a large part of its income to items of high display value such as fashionable apartments, stylish clothing, and greatly overpriced automobiles. Thus, in contrast to the middle classes of other world areas, the Latin American Metropolitan Middle Class apparently has not yet developed an emphasis on savings or a distinctive "middle class ideology."

Although the Urban Proletariat is numerically the dominant segment of the metropolitan centers, it is the least well known of all. The phenomenal growth of Latin American urban centers in the last generation, mainly as a result of migration from rural zones, indicates that a large percentage of the Urban Proletariat may actually be carriers of Peasant, Plantation, or Town subcultures. A study by Lewis of migrants from Tepoztlán to Mexico City (1952) indicates that their ideological culture remains basically unchanged despite the urban setting. Only empirical research will answer the question whether there is a type of Latin American subculture distinct from the Urban Proletariat and different from the subcultures of small towns and rural areas.

III

Whether or not the present typology of subcultures will be of any value in controlling variations and differences in the complexity of Latin American culture and whether it will provide a useful frame of reference for research depends on its operational utility in concrete situations. Its final usefulness over an area as large as the whole of Latin America will, of course, depend on considerably more research and on whether or not the available data can be ordered meaningfully within this framework. But an illustration of the use of this typology in a specific research project may indicate its possible value in the study of complex modern cultures. The research referred to was carried out in the State of Bahia in Brazil in 1950–1951 and comprised the study of three communities, each in a different ecological zone of the state. The communities studied were: Vila Recôncavo, in the sugar-planting area near the coast;

Minas Velhas, an old mining center in the central mountain zone; and Monte Serrat, a community in the arid semidesert of the northeast.* An analysis of the subcultures present in these communities and in the state of Bahia seemed to be most meaningful in describing this sociocultural diversity.

Not all subculture types outlined in this paper will, of course, be present in any particular area of Latin America. In the State of Bahia, the indigenous population was quickly exterminated or assimilated. Thus the subculture types called Tribal Indian and Modern Indian are not present. But throughout the state there are numerous rural agriculturalists, many of whom are descendants of Indians, whose subculture is of the type identified above as Peasant. Throughout the state there are also small towns which are trading and administrative centers with Town subcultures. The coast of Bahia, especially around the Bay of Todos os Santos, where it is known as the Recôncavo, was one of the earliest sites of sugar plantations in Latin America. Here are found both the old-style engenho-type and the new usina-type sugar plantations. And finally in the city of Salvador—the capital and largest metropolitan center of the state—there is a culturally conservative urban upper class preserving many old Brazilian traditions, as well as a large metropolitan proletariat.

Each of the communities in which field research was carried out contains at least two subcultures. The old mining town of Minas Velhas is a trading, manufacturing, and administrative center for a larger community encompassing a number of

* This program was sponsored by the Department of Anthropology of Columbia University and the government of the State of Bahia (Brazil). It was directed by Professor Thales de Azevedo of the University and the author. The research in Vila Recôncavo was carried out by Harry W. Hutchinson (1952; 1957); Minas Velhas was studied by Marvin Harris (1952; 1956); and Monte Serrat by Ben Zimmerman (1952). A fourth study was carried out later by Anthony Leeds (1957) in the cacao producing zone of southern Bahia.

satellite villages inhabited by simple peasant farmers. Monte Serrat contains these same two subcultures: a religious, administrative, and trading town which is visited periodically by the surrounding scattered peasant population. The third community, Vila Recôncavo, contains a town which is inhabited by traders, government employees, a group of fishermen, a few artisans, manual laborers, and a variety of marginal wage earners. It also contains in the rural zone a series of engenho-type plantations, a small usina which still administers its various plantations as separate units (during the transition between the engenho-type and usina-type plantations), and a number of Metropolitan Upper Class families—owners of plantations and of the usina—who participate in community life. The other Metropolitan subcultures (Middle Class and Urban Proletariat) are found in the city of Salvador but were not studied by this research project.* Of the major subculture types found within the State of Bahia, four are represented in the communities of research.

Despite differences deriving from the degree of isolation, from different environments, and from different local historical circumstances, there are many crucial similarities in the Town subcultures of Monte Serrat, Minas Velhas, and Vila Recôncavo on the one hand, and in the Peasant subcultures of these same communities on the other hand. Likewise there are crucial differences between the Peasant and Town subcultures of each community as well as between these subcultures and the Plantation and Metropolitan Upper Class subcultures of Vila Recôncavo. The broad sociocultural differences between subcultures of different types in the Bahia area conform to the criteria upon which this taxonomy of Latin American subcultures was based and have therefore been described above. But

---

* A study of a working-class district was carried out by Thales de Azevedo of the University of Bahia, as a follow-up on our research.

a specific illustration may help to clarify how such a typology can be used to explore additional categories of patterned behavior.

During the period of fieldwork, general elections were held throughout Brazil. There was considerable subcultural regularity in the communities being studied in regard to political behavior during the campaigns and during the election.

Peasant subcultures. There was little or no interest in the elections among the peasant segment of the population in both Minas Velhas and Monte Serrat. On election day in Monte Serrat, political parties sent trucks out to the rural zone to bring peasants to town to vote. The day was treated as an outing by peasants and their families who came to town dressed in their best clothes. They were served free meals by the political party which claimed their vote and whose truck had transported them to town. They voted according to the dictates of an influential townsman; they were motivated by personal loyalty and economic bonds (debts) rather than by strong political feelings or beliefs. Similar behavior was also reported of the peasants in Minas Velhas as well as of other communities with Peasant-type subcultures in which more casual observations were made during the political campaign and the elections.

Town subcultures. The political campaign in both Minas Velhas and Monte Serrat (communities with Peasant and Town subcultures) was intense among the townspeople, yet their interest was focused upon local and state rather than national issues. In both Minas Velhas and Monte Serrat, the townspeople were split by allegiances to opposing political parties. In Monte Serrat each of the principal bars was frequented only by men belonging to one political party; anyone known to have any sympathy for the opposing party would not dare enter the bar of the other. Two public address systems blared forth each day competing with each other in sheer volume and in political promises and accusations. Practically all conversation revolved around the coming elections. In both Minas Velhas and Monte Serrat almost everyone had something at stake; municipal, state, and federal employees were anxious for their jobs, and commercial men and artisans hoped to gain favors from being on the winning side. Even the parish priests were intensely active in the campaign, and their sermons were not free of political propaganda. During the campaign normal social life (visiting among families, dances, and the like) was almost entirely suspended. Election day was a tense and active occasion for the townspeople, most of whom were busy attempting to influence the peasant voter until he actually walked into the polls. Short visits during this period to other Bahian communities made it clear that this intense political activity was typical of Town subculture political behavior.

In the third community that contained a Town subculture, Vila Recôncavo, the political behavior of the town dwellers deviated from that described above as typical of Town subcultures. In Vila Recôncavo, the political scene was dominated by Metropolitan Upper Class families. The local candidate for mayor was a member of one of these families rather than of the town upper class as in the two communities described above. Because of the powerful personal and economic hold which this landed gentry exerted on local affairs, the towns-people were not able to organize an effective opposition and the candidate ran virtually unopposed. The townspeople (commercial men, bureaucrats, artisans, and so forth) put on a weak imitation of the political campaign which took place in Minas Velhas and Monte Serrat, but it was a foregone conclusion that the party of the Metropolitan Upper Class (landed gentry) would win. Thus in regions or areas such as the Recôn-cavo of Bahia State where the town is overshadowed by the surrounding plantations and the communities dominated by a landed gentry, the criteria of intense political activity for Town-type subcultures will be regularly absent.

Engenho Plantation subcultures. As stated above, the community of Vila Recôncavo contained family-owned, engenho-type sugar plantations. During the political campaigns of 1950 little was heard about politics from the workers on these plantations. When asked how they might vote, they were apt to answer, "I don't know, I haven't found out how the patrao will vote," or, "With the patrao, Senhor." For them, election day was a day without work when those who were literate (able to sign their names) went to town to vote as did the plantation owners. Such behavior seemed to be typical of workers on Engenho plantations throughout the State of Bahia.

Usina Plantation subcultures. Although as stated above there was not a large Usina plantation in any of the communities studied intensively in the Bahia area, we were able to observe political behavior in nearby highly industrialized sugar plantations. From the messages painted on walls in red and black paint at night urging the election of one candidate or another (especially of left-wing groups) and from the numerous political posters, it was obvious that political activity was intense among the Usina workers. Far from voting with the administrators, these workers on large industrialized plantations supported the opposing political party. Labor unions exerted considerable influence, and in general the workers were much interested in politics. Furthermore, because much of their political education came from national organizations such as labor unions and Vargas' Brazilian Labor Party (Partido Trabalhista Brasileiro), their interest focused more on national elections than on local and state elections.

Metropolitan Upper Class subcultures. Representatives of the upper class were present in only one of the communities studied, Vila Recôncavo. For this group, political activity on a high level is characteristic and traditional. Most individuals in this class had friends or relatives to whom success or failure at the polls was of the utmost importance. Cousins of important families in Vila Recôncavo were candidates for federal deputy, and one of the candidates for governor was a lifelong friend of most of the members of the same families. In Salvador large, united families from this group were pitted against each other for political control of the state and city. But, as stated above, in Vila Recôncavo, because of the Metropolitan Upper Class families have intermarried, they presented in a sense a united front. Thus the outcome of the election in Vila Recôncavo was easily predicted.

Metropolitan Middle Class and Urban Proletariat subcultures. Little can be said regarding the political behavior of these groups during the 1950 campaigns and elections. It was obvious that political reactions of both groups were emotional and intense, but large-scale quantitative techniques would be necessary to study the political behavior of this large mass of people.

A great number of subcultural regularities which are valid for the area studied might also be pointed out. Material culture, technology, concepts of the cause and cure of disease, work patterns, occupational specialization, settlement patterns, housing, etiquette, speech habits, social ranking, and many other items are variable within the communities but constant within the subcultures of the area. Even the use made of tobacco is regular according to subculture type rather than community: peasant women smoke pipes, town women do not smoke, and Metropolitan Upper Class women smoke cigarettes. Thus a typology of subcultures is an indispensable tool for relating the community to its larger sociocultural context. Such a typology not only lends order to research materials and directs attention to the need for additional comparative data, but it also provides a basis for predicting with reasonable accuracy the reactions of certain segments of the population to new social stimuli. It is therefore utilitarian for both theoretical and applied purposes.

IV

Through a comparison of four Yucatán communities—Tusik, a tribal village of Quintana Roo; Chan Kom, a peasant community; Dzitas, a town on the railroad; and the city of Merida—Redfield concluded in his *The Folk Culture of Yucatán* (1941: 339):

. . . the peasant village as compared with the tribal village, the town as compared with the peasant village, or the city as compared with the town is less isolated, is more heterogeneous; is characterized by a more complex division of labor; has a more completely developed money economy; has professional specialists who are more secular and less sacred; has kinship and godparental institutions that are less well organized and less effective in social control; is correspondingly more dependent on impersonally acting institutions of control, is less religious, with respect to both beliefs and practices of Catholic origin as well as those of Indian origin; exhibits less tendency to regard sickness as resulting from a breach of moral or merely customary rule; allows a greater freedom of action and choice to the individual; and . . . shows a greater emphasis upon black magic as an ascribed cause of sickness.

Except as these differences relate to the regional culture of Yucatán they are also implied in the present taxonomy of subcultures, and it should be noted that six of the subculture types discussed above are carried by the local societies or by segments of the societies studied by Redfield in Yucatán. Thus

Merida would presumably contain subcultures of all three Metropolitan types. Dzitas seems to have both Town and a Peasant types of subculture. Chan Kom, in our terms, would be a community with a Peasant subculture and Dzitas would be representative of our Modern Indian subculture. Although neglected by Redfield, Plantation subculture types are also present in the henequen-producing area of Yucatán (Mintz 1953a:138). Tribal Indian subcultures, as defined above, are no longer present in the peninsula. Thus the present classification is clearly related to Redfield's folk-urban gradient. A fundamental difference exists, however. If the present taxonomy were to be used as the basis of a study of the urban-folk continuum in Latin America, the lines in the gradient would have to consist not of whole communities but of segments of whole communities. In this way one of the most serious defects in the use of the folk culture concept can be circumvented, for, as Lewis has shown for Tepoztlán (1951), the homogeneity of a rural community with respect to its folk characteristics is easily overemphasized when it is the whole local society which is the subject of characterization.

Redfield was primarily interested in cultural change, especially the effects of modern urbanization upon "folk culture" and the resulting "disorganization of the culture, secularization, and individualization," to use his well-known terms. The primary purpose of the present taxonomy is not to analyze the direction and effects of cultural change but to establish categories which may help to orient many additional problems. Many of the subculture types we have been describing are more or less stable features of the Latin American scene. Although individual settlements or large segments of their populations may change rapidly from carriers of one subculture type to another (for example, Indians become mestizos) and although new subculture types have appeared, most of these subculture types have been part of the cultural scene of Latin America since the sixteenth century. They have changed in culture content and in their relative importance to the wider cultural scene, but they have constantly maintained their distinctiveness as variations of Latin American culture and their essential relationships to one another.

Soon after 1500 when the distinctive culture of Latin America began to take form, Modern Indian, Peasant, Town Engenho Plantation, and Metropolitan Upper Class types were already present in the New World. The European conquerors brought with them a strong tradition of urbanism. In their European homelands there were cities, towns, and peasant villages. Large agrarian estates, similar in some ways to the New World plantations, were also present. Furthermore, as is well known, the native civilizations of America also had their cities, their market centers, and their villages and hamlets. The Europeans transplanted to the New World a culture which was already characterized by a number of subcultures analogous to those described for modern Latin America, but in the New World the subcultures were modified in content and in the form of interaction between them.

The Spanish and Portuguese (also the other nationals who controlled more limited areas of Latin America) who were given land grants, encomiendas, or other economic rights in the New World soon established a colonial aristocracy with traditions derived from the feudal aristocratic patterns of their homeland. In the region of native American civilization, these colonial aristocrats supplanted the native ruling class, and in lowland Latin America they dominated the segmented tribal groups and owned African slaves. Although only small numbers of European peasants came to the New World to work the land as they had done in Europe, a few did come, transporting their way of life almost intact. Before long, however, a distinctive Latin American Peasant subculture took form as the various tribal groups of the lowland region came under the influence of missionaries and colonial governments, lost their identity as autochthonous peoples, and borrowed or had forced upon them European culture patterns. Under the impact of Spanish rule, the Indians of the highland regions acquired numerous Spanish culture patterns which fused with aboriginal patterns to form the subculture type called herein Modern Indian. The content of each of these subculture types differed, of course, from that of today, but those of 1600 were the historical antecedents of the contemporary types.

The transition of populations from one subculture type to another still goes on. The Tenetehara, a Tupí-speaking tribe of northern Brazil, for example, still has a culture that is essentially aboriginal and distinct from the culture of the Brazilian nation within the borders of which it happens to live. But the Tenetehara are slowing adopting Brazilian culture patterns; they are being brought into the orbit of the Brazilian commercial system through the sale of palm nuts and because of the increasing necessity to purchase imported and manufactured supplies (Wagley and Galvão 1949). The Tenetehara might now be classed as a Modern Indian subculture. As the process of acculturation continues, they will lose their identity as "distinct people," and their culture will be transformed into that of a Peasant subculture of modern Brazil. Likewise, in Ecuador, Guatemala, Mexico, Peru, and other countries where there are large numbers of people living by Modern Indian subculture patterns, there is a noted trend for such Indians to adopt Peasant patterns (that is, mestizo, ladino, or cholo patterns) and to lose their identity as Indians. In many localities of Latin America both Indians and peasants are still being drawn upon as plantation workers, especially as communal forms of land tenure break down and as commercial agricultural enterprises expand their holdings. In other localities many isolated areas inhabited by peasants are being connected with national markets by roads and other means of communication, and towns are taking form where a small local marketplace once existed. Under similar impulses, small towns are growing in size and in complexity to become veritable cities. And as noted earlier there is a continuing trend for family-owned engenho-type plantations to be welded into large, industrialized usina-type plantations.

All Latin American subcultures are certainly changing under urban and industrial influences, and yet the differences between some of them may remain great for many years to come. The content of Peasant and Metropolitan subcultures in Europe has in both cases changed profoundly during the last five hundred years, but the differences between city dwellers and peasants in almost any European nation are still striking. In the future certain subcultures may diminish in importance or entirely disappear as the people who carry them adopt other culture patterns. Tribal Indian subculture types will probably disappear well within the next hundred years, and Engenho Plantation types are becoming extinct with at least equal rapidity. Modern Indian types, on the other hand, especially where enlightened policies of government assistance prevail, are likely to endure for much longer. Barring wide political upheaval, Peasant, Town, Usina Plantation, and Metropolitan Upper Class subculture types also appear to have long futures ahead of them, while the Metropolitan Middle Class and Urban Proletariat types are just now beginning to emerge.

The changes in content which all these subculture types are undergoing are adequately embraced by the folk-urban transition suggested by Redfield. But any picture of progressive urbanization must take into account the possibility that as the subculture types change toward greater urbanization, most of them do not merge in content, but remain as distinctly defined as ever within the national context. This is true because throughout all the stages of the urbanization of a nation, the city subcultures are not static but rather continue to be the innovators of most of the new features. Furthermore although the rural-urban concept provides us with excellent hypotheses for the general direction of diffusion of new cultural items on a national scale, it does not prepare us for the problem of fundamental structural changes such as the emergence of new subcultures or the realignment of power. To describe the structure of a complex nation and the changes it is undergoing we need a taxonomy of parts such as that which has been tentatively developed in this paper. The emergence of new and the extinction of old sociocultural segments is an aspect of cultural change which the student of complex national cultures cannot afford to neglect.

[IV]

THE PEASANT

THE population of Latin America is predominantly rural. Well over 60 per cent of approximately 200 million Latin Americans are classified as rural in accordance with the census criteria of various countries.* Many Latin Americans live in small towns of less than 3,000 people. Many others work on large pastoral or agricultural establishments such as Argentine cattle estancias; Brazilian coffee fazendas; banana plantations in Caribbean countries such as Costa Rica and Honduras; sugar plantations in Brazil, coastal Peru, and other tropical countries; and other large-scale monocultural farms producing cash crops such as cacao, henequen, and cotton. Perhaps the largest number of these rural Latin Americans, however, are "peasants," that is, "agricultural producers in effective control of land who carry on agriculture as a means of livelihood, not as a business for profit" (Wolf 1956b:1065). They are the Indians living in

This paper originally was written for a symposium on various social sectors of Latin American contemporary society. This symposium was organized by the Joint Committee on Latin America of the Social Science Research Council and the American Council of Learned Societies. It was first published in *Continuity and Change in Latin America*, edited by John J. Johnson (Stanford University Press, 1964).

* Examples of "urban" criteria are: Mexico—populated centers of more than 2,500 inhabitants; Guatemala—places with 2,000 or more inhabitants, and places with 1,500 or more inhabitants if running water service is provided in the houses; Brazil—administrative centers of *municipios* and centers of population of districts, including suburban zones.

scattered homesteads or small hamlets in Mexico, Guatemala, Ecuador, Peru, and Bolivia. They are also the small farmers of Costa Rica, Chile, Colombia, and most other Latin American countries. But they must not be confused with European or North American family farmers because almost everywhere Latin American peasants retain indigenous traditions of swidden or slash-and-burn agriculture. They are usually poor, illiterate, in poor health, out of touch with the modern trends of their nation, and looked down on as rustics by the town and city people. Yet in some countries they have a voice. They are sought out by politicians who realize that, at least potentially, political power is rooted in the peasants. They are the people who stream into urban centers, causing the problems concomitant to rapid and unplanned urban growth. They are also evolving rapidly within their own communities, and becoming an important social and political force on the national scene. They are an important sector of the Latin American population, providing many examples of continuity and change.

THE LATIN AMERICAN PEASANTRY

The peasants of Latin America are perhaps the best-studied segment of the population. Some time ago anthropologists and sociologists became interested in the Indians of Mexico, Guatemala, and Andean South America, who were descendants of the Aztecs, the Mayans, and the Incas. In Brazil and the Caribbean lowlands, scholars were attracted to the study of the survival of African traits among the descendants of slaves. From these humble beginnings, motivated by ethnographic and historical interests (that led to questions such as, What had survived of Mayan culture in Yucatán or Guatemala and of African culture in Haiti or Brazil?), there developed a long series of community studies. As anthropological and sociological theory and technique became more sophisticated, these studies focused increasingly on communities that were considered highly representative of specific subcultures, regions, or nations. The result was a large number of individual community studies and several very persuasive theoretical syntheses of Latin American community life. Robert Redfield's classic work, *The Folk Culture of Yucatán* (1941), stimulated a series of general articles on the relationship of peasants to the larger society of which they are a part.

Latin America is not a particularly fortunate laboratory for these theoretical formulations. It does not have the long cultural and social continuity of Sweden, Greece, India, or West Africa, to cite but a few examples. One cannot trace the development of the Latin American peasantry directly back to the Middle Ages and further back to the Neolithic Age. The Spanish conquest of Mexico, Guatemala, Peru, and other countries and the introduction of Negro slavery were violent revolutions that broke the continuity of New World history more decisively than any political, industrial, or social revolution in the Old World. The Spanish conquest, in its broadest sense, profoundly modified the lives of well over twenty million American aborigines, and slavery transferred at least ten million Negroes to the New World. Everywhere in the countries of Latin America, these two cataclysmic processes created a peasantry that is analogous to the European and even the Asian peasantry only in a formal sense. Its relationship to the local elite is similar to that of its European counterpart, and its land tenure situation is roughly the same; but it is part of a relatively recent society which took form after 1500 without the long continuity of Old World history.

The peasants of Latin America comprise a board spectrum of peoples. They include the rural Indians and mestizos of Mexico, the descendants of the Maya of Guatemala and Yucatán, the Quechua-speaking Indians and Spanish-speaking cholos of Peru and Ecuador, and the caboclos of the Brazilian interior. They nonetheless share certain traits and a position in the national social structure that allow us to classify them generically as Latin American peasants.

First of all, they all live in rural areas that are usually quite removed from the modern national life of their country. In one way or another, they have control over the land they cultivate. They may be members of communal landholding villages, individual land owners, sharecroppers, or squatters on the lands of others. They usually plant subsistence crops such as maize, manioc, potatoes, or wheat, but as a rule they must sell surplus food or cash crops to make ends meet. Some of them are artisans producing home crafts, and some are traders selling local foods and articles at regional markets. Sometimes they must seek seasonal wage labor on plantations because their local economy does not provide an adequate income. The Indians of highland Guatemala work on the coffee fincas, and many caboclos of northeast Brazil go to work on the sugarcane fields of the coast each year to supplement their income.

Unlike tribal people, these Latin American peasants are an integral part of their nation and of their regional, if not national, economic system. In some cases, however, peasants are not even aware of their status as nationals and as participants in a larger economic system. They often think of themselves as members of a separate group who must work for outsiders from time to time. Their point of view is analogous to that of a Mexican bracero going to work on a farm in the United States. This is true of many Indians who seek seasonal employment on plantations in Guatemala, Peru, or Ecuador. Others who are fully aware of their economic and national status may be equally distressed about their need to seek employment outside the community, if it separates them from their families and from their normal sphere of social relations.

Generally speaking, all Latin American peasants share what might be called a colonial, Iberian culture. This is a New World culture chiefly based on Iberian institutions and patterns of thought, but mixed with traits retained from the American Indian, from the African slave, or from both, depending on the region involved. The peasant's way of life was set in the early colonial period, when the Spandiards and the Portuguese actively attempted, with only partial success, to remake the Indian and the Negro in their own image. Since then most Latin American peasants have lived in relative social and cultural isolation. Only recently have they been aware of, and subject to, the larger society of which in fact they have always been a part. Latin American peasants are Catholics, but their Catholicism has absorbed so many elements of African belief, the American Indian religion, and European folklore from the sixteenth and seventeenth centuries, that it often seems strange to more orthodox Catholics of the great metropolitan centers.

The peasants' ideal pattern of behavior, their motivations, and their world view are "conservative"—that is, they reflect periods in the past when they were more attuned first to the colonial, and then to the national way of life. Their agricultural methods are "primitive," and peasant markets primarily involve local products and transactions between local producers and local buyers. They tend to retain old, traditional institutions and customs. They take seriously the obligations of the compadrazgo system; they join and serve in the cofradías or irmandades (religious brotherhoods) of their own communities; and they fulfill their vows to the saints. Whatever small economic surplus they have is often drained by expenditures in their local prestige system, which involves the financing of fiestas and time off from productive activities for religious and public service to the community. Wherever we go in Latin America the peasant is a recognizable social type, although he may share many characteristics with other depressed groups such as hacienda workers, or even inhabitants of newly formed city slums.

This generalized characterization of the Latin American peasantry hardly does justice to reality; it does not take into account the important variations in the peasant populations of different Latin American countries and regions. The peasants of Mexico or Peru are very different from the caboclos of Brazil, and the Indian peasants of Mexico, Guatemala, Ecuador, Peru, or Bolivia differ from the non-Indian peasants of those same countries, although, as noted above, all these groups do share common characteristics and problems. Broadly speaking one must take into account at least two subtypes, the Indian and the mestizo peasants, although a much larger series of subtypes may be distinguished.*

Throughout the highlands of Mexico, Guatemala, Ecuador, Peru, Bolivia, and to a certain extent in Colombia, a large number of Indian villages managed to weather the Spanish conquest and to reorganize along lines imposed by the Spanish rulers. Characteristically these free Indian communities were found in high mountainous areas where the land was marginal and ordinarily too high for cash crops. Under Spanish rule, and perhaps even before, the community was a landholding corporation. Although individuals and families might exploit the land (and indeed they usually did), ultimate title belonged to

---

* Elsewhere (Wagley and Harris 1955:428–51) the terms "Modern Indian" and "Peasant" were used for these same subtypes or, as we called them, "subcultures." Eric Wolf (1955:452–71) has termed them "corporate" and "open" peasant types, terms derived from the structure of the communities in which each type characteristically lives. I agree with Wolf that both types are "peasants," and thus I have chosen to use the terms "Indian peasant" and "mestizo peasant" in the present paper. They differ from one another both in culture content and in terms of their respective positions within the national social structure. Richard N. Adams (1956:881–907) has provided a much more refined set of subtypes for Central America.

the community. Such Indian peasant communities were closed because members belonged to them by birth and married within their own group. Each of these closed corporate communities regarded itself as a separate and distinct entity. Its saints were local saints and were unlike those of other communities. Men were obligated to participate in local political and religious affairs. The social world of the individual in such communities was bound intimately to his local group, although he might have been forced to leave it periodically to work on a coffee finca, on a sugarcane plantation, or in the city in order to supplement his income. As stated above, these corporate villagers were usually Indians. Their habitual language was Nahautl, Zapotec, Maya, Quechua, Aymara, or some other aboriginal tongue; this was another barrier separating them not only from the Spanish-speaking nationals of their countries but sometimes from one another. As a general rule, the people of each community wore a distinctive costume; it was easy to recognize a man or woman from Santiago Chimaltenango (Guatemala), Chamula (Mexico), Otavalo (Ecuador), or a thousand other communities.

In the nineteenth century, under the guise of ideological liberalism, Latin American governments passed a number of laws aimed at the substitution of private property for communal holdings. Many Indian communities lost their lands and became integral parts of large haciendas, thus in a sense disappearing as free peasant groups. Other communities divided the communal lands among their members (sometimes preserving a small area of common lands), but retained a strong taboo on alienation of land to outsiders. This practice allowed them to survive as free Indian villages into the twentieth century. Still others, often aided by the *indigenista* groups and the rise of twentieth-century liberal thought, were able to retain or even reestablish their communal holdings, allocating parcels to their members periodically. These, of course, are the groups that today most markedly retain their characteristics as Indian peasants separate from the nation of which they are a part.

The mestizo peasant community, on the other hand, has always been more closely identified with and related to the nation. Mestizo peasants generally, but not always, speak the national language, either Spanish or Portuguese. They are the rural mestizos of Mexico, the rural ladinos of Guatemala, the cholos of Ecuador and Peru, and the caboclos, tabareus, caipiras, or matutos of Brazil. Biologically such people may be Indians, Europeans, Negroes, or mixtures in various degrees of the three racial groups. Their biological heritage is not important. What is important is the fact that they are consciously aware of their identity as members of a nation. They participate in national affairs as closely as their isolation, their limited income, and their literacy will permit. They tend to look outward to the region and the nation rather than inward to their little community. If they are literate and if there are elections, they sometimes vote and participate in political affairs, as they have in Bolivia since 1953. Although they usually marry locally, as most country folk do, there is no rule of endogamy as in the corporate-type Indian communities. They wear western-style clothes, although these may be old-fashioned or ragged. They play soccer and, in some Caribbean countries, baseball. They respect and celebrate the religious and civic holidays of their nation, and they are familiar with its heroes, both past and present.

As Eric Wolf has pointed out (1955:461), open-community or mestizo peasants are more closely tied to the wider economic system than are Indian peasants. Many of them live by selling cash crops, which constitute from 50 to 75 per cent of their total production. In the lowlands of the Caribbean, they grow cacao and bananas for sale. In many cases they grow coffee or tobacco, crops that lend themselves both to large and small holdings. In Brazil, these peasants produce manioc, flour, maize, and other food staples for sale at local markets.* But, as noted above, the Latin mestizo peasant is not analogous to the European farmer or peasant. In the transfer of culture from the Old World to the New, the European mixed-farming tradition was somehow lost. The Latin American peasant seldom combines agriculture with stock raising. He may have a few chickens, a pig, and perhaps a cow or two, but meat is a rare item on his table. He seldom makes butter, cheese, or any of the common farm products of Europe and North America at home. To buy such foods as well as other necessities, the Latin American peasant must have some sort of surplus to sell at market—or he must sell his labor on plantations or in the city.

As stated above, the mestizo peasants share some characteristics with Indian peasants, but they differ in many important respects. Mestizo peasants are generally just as poor as Indian peasants; they are often just as illiterate; their health is no better. But unlike Indian peasants, they prefer to accumulate valuables or land rather than spend their surplus income on service to the community. They are also more commercial; almost any mestizo home may also be a shop with a few eggs, some matches, soft drinks, or other items for sale. Likewise they are aware of and eager for material objects of all kinds (transistor radios, better clothes, better housing, and the like). They are more apt to migrate in the hope of acquiring such objects and of improving their miserable rural conditions. They seem to have a stronger desire for education for their children than the Indians. Land is, of course, owned privately,

---

* One might also include as mestizo peasants those rural groups that collect palm nuts, gather wild rubber, raise livestock, and fish, when these activities are performed outside the orbit of large estates and are combined with subsistence agriculture.

if there is title at all. Mestizo peasants show less cohesion or esprit de corps among themselves; in fact, as we shall see, mestizo peasants usually belong to a community split by class, racial, and even political lines.

THE PEASANT AND THE COMMUNITY

Thus far, Indian and mestizo peasants have been discussed as if they lived apart in small, self-contained communities. In reality, few peasant villages are fullfledged communities, if one defines a community as the minimal local unit that can carry and transmit a culture (Arensberg 1961:253). Several writers have stressed the structural dependence of all peasants on the town, the city, and the larger society (Kroeber 1948; Redfield 1953; Foster 1953:153 ff.; Wolf 1955:461). Few Indian corporate groups are actually full communities, but some closely approach the abstract model described above. Most Indian villages also include mestizos who are not only peasants, but also traders, bureaucrats, and artisans. The non-Indians who live in Indian villages may be considered outsiders despite the fact that they often serve as teachers, government officers, and commercial traders, and in other capacities essential to the local society. Furthermore these quasi-Indian communities are often dependent to a large extent on the mestizo towns and cities around them.

The case for mestizo peasant groups functioning as a community seems even less valid. Lacking the unity derived from communal land holdings and from taboos against the alienation of land to outsiders, mestizo peasants generally form neighborhoods or a social stratum within a larger community, centered upon a town that serves as their market and bureaucratic center. Most of them live in communities that also include nonpeasant storekeepers, government officials, artisans, and landowners who do not work the land themselves. Sometimes mestizo peasants may be part of a local community that also includes a hacienda or plantation on which they seek periodic work for wages. One community may include in addition to mestizo peasants, plantation or hacienda colonos (permanent wage workers), middle-class elements, and even a landowning aristocracy, as did Vila Recôncavo in the sugarcane-growing region of northern Brazil (Hutchinson 1957). Or a community may be composed of Indian and mestizo peasants as well as of middle-class town folk, as was San Luis Jilotepeque in eastern Guatemala (Gillin 1951; Tumin 1952).

Thus it is difficult to speak of a homogeneous corporate Indian peasant community or a homogeneous mestizo peasant community, although examples of both may be found. However it is possible to think of these two peasant types independently of the communities in which they live. An Indian peasant may live in a corporate community, and his behavior will be conditioned by the current social sanctions of the community; yet, as a rule, if he migrates to a plantation, to a mestizo town, or to the city, he does not change his behavior abruptly or drastically. He may no longer spend any surplus he may acquire on community fiestas, for example; but he is apt to look back to his community to celebrate its saints' days, and in a hundred other ways to behave like the Indian peasant he is. Similarly, the mestizo peasant who has migrated to the city tends to retain his rural behavior patterns as far as this is possible in the urban environment. These two abstract models, the Indian peasant and the mestizo peasant, whether they are considered in terms of homogeneous communities or of social types, can be useful in discussing recent social and economic changes and future trends in the peasant sector of Latin American society.

Although such abstract models as Indian peasants and mestizo peasants can be useful tools of description and analysis, the social anthropologist is most at home when working with concrete cases, namely specific local communities, attempting as he does to relate his community to a broader frame of reference. For the purpose of this paper, two communities—Santiago Chimaltenango, a community of Indian peasants in Guatemala, and Itá in the Brazilian Amazon region, in which mestizo peasants predominate—will be examined in some detail.* Neither community is a truly representative example of its respective peasant subtype. Both are somewhat outside the mainstream of social change among the peasantry of their respective nations. Perhaps this is advantageous because they reflect basic changes in a less dramatic manner, and their future is portended by the changes that are taking place more rapidly elsewhere.

SANTIAGO CHIMALTENANGO: THE INDIAN PEASANTS

Santiago Chimaltenango is a community of Mam- (Mayan-) speaking Indians situated high in the Cuchamatán mountains of northwestern Guatemala. In 1937 it had a population of approximately 1,500 people. About 900 of these lived in the pueblo, the seat of the county-like *municipio;* the others lived in isolated homesteads or small hamlets (*aldeas*) scattered over the countryside. It was almost a homogeneous Indian peasant community, for only three families (37 people) classified as ladinos (non-Indians) lived there. All Chimaltecos spoke Mam habitually, although a small minority, chiefly men, also spoke Spanish. They regarded themselves as different

* The author carried out intensive field research in both communities many years ago. Field research in Santiago Chimaltenango was done in 1937 (Wagley 1941; and Wagley 1949). The research in Itá was spread over several periods from 1942 to 1948, but the longest period was in 1948 (see Wagley 1953). A short revisit to Santiago Chimaltenango was made in 1956, and one to Itá in 1962. It must not be thought that either of these revisits was in any way a restudy, but they did allow a quick eyewitness view of some obvious changes and trends in the communities in question.

from the people of San Juan Atitán and San Pedro Necta—
communities bordering their territory—as well as from the Indians of all other municipios and from the non-Indian nationals of Guatemala. They wore a distinctive costume which
set them off from other Indians and from ladinos. With rare
exceptions, they married only among themselves. Individuals
who had entered the community through marriage were considered outsiders for life, and their children were known as the
offspring of mixed marriages.

In the nineteenth century the lands of Chimaltenango were
held in common, but by 1937 all tracts, except a very high and
rugged piece of *ejido* (common land) had been reduced to
individual tenure. Yet at that time community sanctions
against selling land to outsiders were still strong, and the community retained its corporate character to a large extent. There
was a marked difference, however, in the size of individual
holdings, which ranged from over 500 *cuerdas*° to less than
ten. Most landholdings were so small that men had to seek
wage labor from more fortunate fellow villagers or from coffee
fincas to provide for their families. Each year a few families
who were landless or whose plots of land were so small that
they provided little income remained premanently on the
fincas as colonos. Such people, living away from their community, became in time what has been called "transitional Indians"—people of intermediate status between the "traditional
Indian" of the community and the ladino (Whetten 1961:76 ff.).

Chimaltenango also retained its traditional political and religious hierarchy, with *principales* (elders), alcaldes (mayors),
regidores (town councilmen), and others, although at the time
these Indian officials were not recognized by the Guatemalan
federal government. Most males served at least one year in
these public offices without remuneration, donating approxi-

° A *cuerda* is 70 square feet; there are 9.2 cuerdas to the acre.

mately half their time during the year. Many served several
years, rising with age through the hierarchy. The expenditures
of office and the time off from productive work acted as economic leveling factors that reduced the accumulated wealth of
the individual. The officials were selected each year by the
principales, who had themselves served in several important
offices. A man's financial status, his age, and his record in lower
offices were important criteria in these selections.

Political life in a Western sense did not exist in 1937. The
Guatemalan dictator, Jorge Ubico, was a face in a picture that
hung in the town hall. People were subject to "vagrancy laws"
requiring them to give proof of fulltime agricultural or wage
activities—or be subjected to labor on the roads. A tax was
levied on the family sweatbath, but it was seldom collected.
The ladino officials were irritants to community cohesion, but
their intrusion into community life was minimal. Recourse to
such officials took place only if the efforts of the Indian officials
failed.

In 1937 all Chimaltecos were Catholics in the local sense of
the term, and religion was a community affair fostering considerable esprit de corps and cohesion. Catholic saints and the
"Owners of the Mountains" (aboriginal deities) were wor-
shipped equally; prayers and ceremonies in honor of the saints
and the aboriginal deities were led by native priests, the
chimans, who had a knowledge of the Mayan calendar system
and of the appropriate prayers and rituals. A Catholic priest
came perhaps once a year, chiefly for the baptism of children
—the only sacrament of the Church almost universally received in Santiago Chimaltenango.

National institutions were already impinging on the isolation
of Santiago Chimaltenango in 1937. There was a school for
boys and one for girls in the pueblo-center, but few families
sent their children to them. With minor exceptions, Chi-

maltecos were farmers specializing in maize production. They sold their surplus at local Indian markets, or to ladino merchants in the city of Huehuetenango. They were subjected to national fluctuations in price, and thus participated in the national economic system. Yet in 1937 Santiago Chimaltenango retained its identity as an almost homogeneous Indian peasant community to a remarkable degree.

By 1956 Santiago Chimaltenango had changed both internally and in relation to the nation. In two decades Guatemala had witnessed the fall of the Ubico dictatorship, the relatively democratic government of Juan José Arévalo (which reorganized the municipal structure), and, finally, the rise and overthrow of the left-wing regime of Jacob Arbenz. In the years following the fall of Ubico in 1944, there was an official interest in Indian affairs, an attempt at agrarian reform, and an intrusion of national politics into the peasant communities. National programs in public health and education, often with United States aid, were begun in Santiago Chimaltenango. The social changes that had occurred in this one community were similar to those taking place even more drastically in other Guatemalan Indian communities, and in broad terms they were similar to those that have taken place in similar groups throughout Latin America.

The total population of Santiago Chimaltenango grew appreciably between 1940 and 1950,* approximately at the same rate (25.6 per cent) as the total population of Guatemala during this period. This population growth, which in itself would have meant less land per capita, was by 1956 combined with a trend for the villagers to sell plots of land to ladinos and to Indians of neighboring municipios. Population expansion and land diminution forced more villagers to migrate permanently to coffee fincas or to the cities seeking work. Simultaneously,

* The 1950 census records about 1,800 people.

the sale of land to outsiders brought individuals into the community who were largely unversed in community traditions such as service in the politico-religious hierarchy, celebration of saints' days, and the local norms of interpersonal relations. The shortage of land and the changing pattern of land tenure in such corporate Indian peasant communities have the dual effect of forcing many individuals into new social and economic systems and of destroying the community's cultural and ideological homogeneity. This is a basic trend working slowly toward the "ladinoization" of whole communities (Whetten 1961:77).

Other changes resulted indirectly from the change in land-tenure pattern in Santiago Chimaltenango. The outsiders brought national politics into the community. Political activity was felt in the village as early as 1944, when the villagers voted solidly for one presidential candidate, Arévalo, who had promised to reestablish them as a separate municipio.* Arévalo's regime was at first "democratic in orientation and program and solicitous of bringing the Indian component of Guatemala into national life in a meaningful social and cultural manner" (M. Nash 1957:102). But, as political life in the nation became intensified with the appearance of a multitude of political parties and the rise of active left-wing movements, political strife began to be felt even in this isolated community. Political parties and labor unions throughout the country became active not only among the ladino population, but also among the Indians (Whetten 1961:312–22). Some Chimaltecos were driven to Guatemala City in trucks to take part in gigantic *campesino* rallies, and in 1956 Indians were pointed out to me as "Communists."

* For a time during the Ubico regime, Santiago Chimaltenango was attached to San Pedro Necta. The restoration of separate status was a major aim of community policy, and was achieved in 1946 during Arévalo's presidency. See Juan de Dios Rosales in Wagley (1949:133–34).

This intrusion of national politics and the concepts of Western elective democracy proved upsetting to the traditional community government. The alcalde and several of the regidores were now elected by popular vote. The man elected as alcalde was an Indian and acceptable to the principales who had formerly selected this officer. But both this alcalde and the "first" regidor refused to carry out the religious ceremonies traditionally incumbent upon such officers. Another elected regidor had never served in any lower office of the politico-religious hierarchy. He was, in fact, a "party man" much too young for the office. The more conservative members of the community feared punishment from God as a result of these infringements. Such political factions had not as yet divided Santiago Chimaltenango seriously, but the process was underway.

In other corporate Indian communities, the intrusion of politics had already taken a more serious character, especially in those communities which contained a larger ladino population (Adams 1957:1–54). In some communities young Indian men fully aware of national party politics were elected to office and ignored the traditional powers of the principales and the old hierarchy (Nash 1957:30). In others, ladinos manipulated the electoral system without regard to the local system (Ewald 1957:20–21). Much of this political activity in the Indian communities ended with the overthrow of the Arbenz government in 1954, but the stability of the traditional politico-religious community system had already been irrevocably disturbed. Today as never before in Latin America, national politics are being felt in these formerly isolated and inward-looking communities.

By 1956 the larger society had also begun to intrude upon the religious life of Santiago Chimaltenango, bringing factionalism to what had been a remarkably united community. There were fifty to sixty Evangélicos (Protestants) who had built a temporary church.° Furthermore, North American Maryknoll Fathers had established themselves in San Pedro Necta, only ten kilometers away and were active in Chimaltenango. They considered the traditional Catholicism of Chimaltenango to be "pagan" and condemned the activities of the confradías, the use of alcohol in ceremonials, and the prayers at mountain shrines. These missionary priests evidently attempted to maintain close control over the community, teaching people to become orthodox Catholics and prohibiting the chimans to carry out their ceremonies in the church. Even older persons who were old friends of the author were secretive about *costumbre* (traditional ritual). The orthodox Catholic group were said to go to confession, to attend Mass, and to be married in the church. The community was thus divided into three religious factions: traditional Indian Catholics, orthodox Catholics, and Protestants. The Chimalteco religious experience during the last two decades can be generalized to include all of Guatemala, and perhaps Latin America as a whole.

The development of public services has contributed further to the awareness of the national scene and to the loss of internal unity in Indian communities. In 1937 Santiago Chimaltenango maintained communications with the state capital through weekly messengers on foot. By 1956 there was a telephone that connected the town hall with the capital and neighboring municipalities. Motor roads had not reached the village, but the Pan American Highway was only a few kilometers away, and jeeps had already come over the mountain trails into the village center. The federal government, with

° June Nash (1960:49–53) discusses the effect of Protestantism on the folk Catholic *cofradía* system in the Guatemalan community of Cantel and the fact that "the Protestant sects drew their younger and more alert members into a network of social relations which was national in scope" (p. 50). See also Harry S. McArthur (1961:63).

United States aid, had installed a water system that replaced the open springs and the fountain in the central plaza. Some houses had water in their kitchens, but most were served by conveniently located public outlets. Many families had privies in 1956; they were unknown in 1937. The market place had been roofed to protect customers and merchants during the heavy rains. The Chimaltenango school had been enlarged and three schools had been built in the rural districts. The number of teachers had grown from two to six, two of whom had attended special courses on the problems of teaching Indians offered by an international organization. Although as late as 1950 almost 90 per cent of the school-aged children in Guatemala did not attend school (Arias B. 1961:16), the opportunities for education in Santiago Chimaltenango were infinitely better than in 1937. The inhabitants were interested in schools and many more children were attending them.

The changes in Santiago Chimaltenango between 1937 and 1956 were not dramatic, primarily because the community is a rather isolated one. But the forces of change were at work in a more intense form in other isolated areas; few corporate Indian peasant communities survive in Mexico and each year the Indian peasants come closer to resembling the mestizo peasants. In Ecuador and Peru, language barriers and caste-like social barriers divide the Indian peasants from the mestizo peasants, as well as from other sectors of the population; but even in these countries, better communications, frequent migration to coastal plantations, and intrusive national institutions and politics are increasingly involving the Indian in national life. And, in Bolivia, the Indian peasant or so-called campesino is now the locus of considerable political power (Patch 1960:108–76).

Despite all this, it is commonly observed that the Indian is the most conservative element in Latin American society. The tenacity with which he clings to traditional ways of life continues to amaze observers. Ruben Reina, for example, in his study of the Indian peasants of Santa Cruz Chinautla, which is located just nine miles from Guatemala City, concludes: "Chinautlecos remain in spite of political or non-political orientations with Chinautla as the locus of their world view." He goes on to say, "It appears that Guatemala City has not seriously influenced the mode of Chinautla. Actually, the city is important only as it offers services instrumental in the preserving of the traditional ways" (Reina 1960:85). During the Arévalo regime before Reina's study, the Indian peasants of Chinautla had received land that allowed them to reestablish their traditional fiesta patterns and to regain to some extent their economic independence.

William Stein describes a similar situation among the Indian peasants of Hualcán in the Andes of central Peru. About half of the men of Hualcán own enough land to be independent of the surrounding haciendas. But many Indian landowners must supplement their income by day labor in nearby towns and on the haciendas. A large proportion of the people of Hualcán are forced to migrate to the coast, where they work on large sugar plantations for periods ranging from a few weeks to years. Most of them, however, ultimately return to Hualcán, especially those that have earned a "stake" with which to buy land or animals. Motor roads and the railroad make the coastal plantations easy to reach. These outside contacts and the frequent migration to the coast have set off a series of social changes in Hualcán; yet Hualcán retains most of the qualities of an Indian peasant community. Those Hualcainos who accumulate any economic surplus derived from agriculture or outside wage labor choose to expend it on the community prestige system of fiestas and in greater participation in the politico-religious system (Stein 1957:19; Stein 1961:18–21). In a sense, the income from outside wage labor allows the people of Hualcán to maintain their traditional institutions and values, and to remain relatively insulated from national society.

As long as Indian peasants can retain control in one way or another over their minuscule plots, and particularly if they receive additional land—they will resist change. This will be especially true as long as the alternative offered them is bare subsistence as second-class citizens in the larger society. Curiously, this conservatism, born in a large part of a self-protective separatism and of the need of the *haciendados* to have a readily available pool of free labor, owes much to the idealistic indigenista movements and, surprisingly, to the agrarian-reform programs of various governments, ineffectual as most of them have been. Because of the additional land made available to Indian peasants, the process of integration of the communities into national life seems to have been delayed.*

On the other hand, governmental land-reform programs also mean increased encroachment of outside influences on Indian community life. Restored land generally must be registered, and it must be used, at least theoretically, in a manner that conforms with federal codes. Agronomists, educators, and other non-Indians inevitably become part of community life under such circumstances. Furthermore, unless such land-reform programs are more drastic and provide increasing amounts of land, their stabilizing effect upon Indian peasant communities can only be temporary. They provide a solution for the present generation, but as the population grows (and it is growing), the man-land ratio will fall again. People will continue to be forced out of their communities to seek em-

* Reina (1960:65). It should not be thought that I am arguing against agrarian and land-tenure reform. It is perhaps the single most needed change in Latin American society. Unless it is thorough and sweeping, however, it will not solve fundamental problems and might have some strange side effects.

ployment on plantations and in cities (Wolf 1962:198 and
Reina 1960:102). The trend, then, seems apparent. In the long
run the Indian peasant will disappear from the Latin American
scene, however slow the process. Communities with collective
land-tenure systems may be formed under revolutionary governments, as they have been in Bolivia. In time these communities will not resemble the traditional, endogamous, inward-
looking corporate Indian communities of the highlands of
Central and South America that have persisted from the
colonial period into the present. They will be communities of
people fully aware of their status as members of a nation.

ITÁ: A MESTIZO PEASANT COMMUNITY

Itá is a small town and a large county-like municipality,
located in the lower Amazon Valley in the state of Pará,
Brazil.* Like Santiago Chimaltenango, it is an isolated community where social and economic change has been slow and
where national crises are felt only in attenuated forms. Yet
many of the trends current among Latin American mestizo
peasants are to be found there.

In 1948 the town of Itá had approximately 500 people and
was the seat of a local administrative unit almost as large as
the state of Rhode Island, with a population of about 5,000.
Not all of these people could properly be called members of
the Itá community, however. The community was restricted to
about 2,000 people who lived in the rural neighborhoods adjacent to the little town. These were the people who looked to
the town as the center of their economic, social, and religious
life. Individuals and families in more remote rural neighborhoods turned to other small nuclei. Like most open communities, Itá is not sharply defined. It is similar in many respects
to the market-town centered communities of the rural United

* Itá is a fictitious name for a real town. (See Wagley, *Amazon Town*.)

States. The residents of Itá and surrounding neighborhoods are quite conscious of being members of a single community, but in certain respects they are not sure where the community's boundaries begin and end.

Physically, the majority of the inhabitants of Itá are mestizos in the broadest sense of the term. A few are phenotypically white or Negroid, and some seem to be Amerindian in physical type; but most are mixtures in varying degrees of these three racial types. Most, but not all, of the people of Itá are peasants. In town, there are government officials serving the municipal, state, and federal governments. There are also tradesmen and a few artisans. Some Itá citizens earn their living entirely from manual labor. In the rural neighborhoods dependent upon Itá, there are many individuals who earn their living entirely from the collection of wild rubber. If the definition of the term "peasant" set forth above were strictly adhered to, only about one-third of the rural population of Itá might be regarded as peasants. These are the people who are fulltime agriculturalists planting manioc, corn, and other garden products for their own use and for sale at the local market. The majority of the rural population combine agriculture with collecting.

In Itá the line between the peasant-planter and the collector of products for sale is a matter of degree—of the percentage of time spent on one or the other activity. Economic activities, furthermore, may vary from year to year; depending on the prices paid for rubber and food products, the same family may emphasize one or the other at different times. This same phenomenon holds true for all of Latin America. Mestizo peasants are often at the same time agriculturalists producing food for their own use and for sale, collectors of native products, fishermen, wage laborers, and artisans. But, as noted earlier, they share a peasant-type subculture that is mainly agrarian in focus, and they are isolated from the literate mainstream of national life.

Itá peasants do not form a community apart from that of nonpeasants. In fact, Itá contains at least two social classes—a town white-collar elite and a town and rural lower class, of which the peasants are an important segment. This is generally true of communities containing mestizo peasants throughout Brazil and in most of Latin America. Such communities might best be termed "town-peasant communities" to indicate their characteristic internal subculture and class differentiation. But despite this internal differentiation, the two classes in communities like Itá share a diffuse but ever-present feeling of identity. They are all Itaenses, while in Santiago Chimaltenango only the Indians are Chimaltecos, and the ladinos are considered outsiders merely residing within the community. Such town-peasant communities, divided as they are by lines of social class and by differences in wealth, lack the strong esprit de corps of Indian peasant communities. People are not so tied to the soil, and they are more outward-looking and sensitive to the national trends.

Unlike so many Indian peasants throughout the Americas, the residents of Itá considered themselves Brazilians in the full sense of the term. Everyone in the community spoke Portuguese. Although the great majority of them were illiterate and therefore could not vote, they were nonetheless aware of and interested in political events. The peasant sector of the community had vague ideas about the size and complexity of their nation. They knew something of its national political figures, its national heroes, past and present, and its national symbols such as the flag and the Seventh of September (Independence Day). They shared with the townsfolk an intense interest in soccer, and with the townspeople they celebrated such Brazilian festivals as St. John's Day, Carnival, and the local community saint's day (St. Benedict's). Their ideal patterns of behavior, which they seldom managed to live up to, were those of the local elite. All of them felt that they ought to be married according to the civil law and the Church, but many of them were not, for one reason or another. They aspired to the traditional Brazilian forms of religion, of family life, of etiquette. Both the peasants and the townspeople, however, retained in varying degrees a belief in concepts of American Indian origin, such as the treatment of illness by the *pagé* (shaman). The peasants of Itá were interested in schools for their children and eager for them to be as well trained as the better-educated Itaenses, whom they respected. In 1948 the town had only one government-supported school, with two teachers. Only sixty-one students attended it. And, in the rural zones, there was but one school with an average attendance of twenty to twenty-five pupils.

The mestizo peasant of Itá, like his counterparts throughout Latin America, shares the ignorance and poverty of the Indian peasant. His agriculture is often just as primitive. His agricultural techniques are not far removed from those inherited from the American Indian. In Itá peasants do not plant coffee, cacao, bananas, or sugarcane as cash crops, as do mestizo peasants in other parts of Brazil and Latin America; but they sell manioc flour and wild rubber, hides, timbó vine (used as a base for insecticides), and other native products in order to buy manufactured articles and other necessities such as kerosene. Like peasant producers of cash crops elsewhere, they are vulnerable to the rise and fall of prices, which they do not understand. They value the accumulation of property. They are less inclined than Indian peasants to gain prestige from the community by spending their surplus on community service or feasting a saint.

Itá peasants control the land on which they live and work, but few have outright title to the land. In the eyes of the law, they are squatters, occupying land to which either traders or absentee landlords have some sort of title. Unlike mestizo peasants in many parts of Latin America, the peasants of Itá do not have to give days of labor as rent for their land. They are, however, generally tied by debt to certain traders to whom they must sell their products and from whom they must buy their necessities. Each has a patrão (boss), a person to whom he is tied by debt, land-rent obligations, and traditional personal ties. Throughout Latin America, this patrão (Portuguese) or patrón (Spanish) system relating the mestizo peasant to the landowner, the trader, the employer, or the political boss has survived as an important relationship.

In 1962, although calm and orderly compared to other places in Brazil, Itá was feeling the pressures of national economic and political instability.* There had never been much food in Itá, but there was a shortage of some basic foodstuffs such as rice, beans, and sundried beef. Rampant inflation was upsetting the local credit system. Storekeepers and rural traders did not want to sell merchandise to agriculturalists or rubber gatherers in June and wait until December to be paid in produce whose price would have risen tremendously. Business, consequently, was in the doldrums. Traders did not solicit new customers, and in fact some of them were concealing their wares so as not to attract credit buyers. Once the debt-credit system failed to function normally, the total commerce of the

* In 1962, the cruzeiro had fallen from 300 to 600 to the dollar, and the nation was wavering between presidential and parliamentary systems of government, an issue settled in January 1963 by a plebiscite in favor of a presidential system. In the state of Rio de Janeiro, there had been riots resulting from food shortages. Peasant unrest was constantly reported from the arid northeastern region of the country.

region was jeopardized to the extent that it theoretically could have ground to a halt.

Social and economic changes were immediately discernible in Itá. For example, the population of the town had doubled between 1948 and 1962. There were more than a thousand people in the town. Where there had been three streets parallel to the river, in 1962 there were four, and a fifth was forming. Itá's population expansion reflects the remarkable growth of the Brazilian national population, but it is also the result of a staging process of rural-urban migration, by which rural Brazilians in ever-increasing numbers are migrating to major cities after first living in small towns such as Itá.

"The rural caboclos," the author was informed, "want to move to town." They are "disillusioned" (*desiludido* was the exact term) by prices paid for rubber and other native products of Amazonia and by the difficulties involved in educating their children and receiving adequate health protection. The people from the countryside are indeed moving to town. They are planting gardens along the new road that penetrates inland from the river. In the town they have a school for their children and enjoy the protection offered by a federal health clinic. They have the luxury of electric lights. They like the general *movimento*—the noise of the radios, the daily buying in the few stores, the political campaigns, the gossip, and other business of town life. By 1962 the local economy in Itá could hardly support a larger urban population. Under present circumstances, there is a limit to the amount of arable land that can be worked by agriculturalists living in town and walking to their fields. There are only a few private employers offering wage labor, and highly sought-after employment on the public works projects (a small hospital and the clearing of an airstrip) is quite limited. There is no industry at all. Thus it is clear that within a short time peasant migrants to the town will be induced to move along to the city, to be replaced by others from the rural zone. The Amazonian cities Belém and Manaus are growing more rapidly than the backcountry and have large shantytowns of recently arrived peasants.

Although this process of emigration to the city is discernible in Itá, it does not reach the same proportions as in northeastern and southern Brazil, in central Peru, in Ecuador, and in other regions of Latin America. The situation of Itá, however, helps us to understand that mestizo peasants do not usually go directly to the great cities. They migrate to plantations that grow coffee, sugarcane, bananas, and other cash crops. They move into small towns from the surrounding rural zones. Then they go to cities and swell the shantytowns.

A great majority of the Latin American population is in the lower age levels. Itá and other Brazilian small towns seem literally to swarm with children. It cannot be stated as fact that mestizo peasants are increasing more rapidly than any other sector of the Latin American population, but in all probability they are. Not only are mestizo peasants multiplying rapidly, but they aspire to a better life. For example, they want their children to have some education. In Itá, as in most town-peasant communities, the educational facilities are swamped. The 1948 school building was still the only educational establishment to be found at Itá in 1962. But then there were nine teachers instead of two. There were over three hundred pupils rather than sixty-one. Furthermore, there were four schools instead of one in the rural zones of the community. These schools offered only four years of primary education. In order to provide as many children as possible with some schooling, they functioned in five shifts of two hours each between seven A.M. and seven P.M. The teachers were better trained, but they were not better paid in terms of their buying power. With only two hours per day of classes six days a week, it is doubtful if the education received in 1962 was any better than that received in 1948. Although more mestizo peasants than ever before are being exposed to formal schooling, the illiteracy rate seems to remain stable. Illiteracy, of course, extends beyond the peasant groups to the towns, plantations, and cities.

In 1962 Itá's communications with the outside world were markedly improved over those of 1948. There was an airstrip (called magnificently the "Municipal Airport") at which "air taxis" landed from time to time. A commercial airline flying amphibian planes made unscheduled stops on the river. Boat traffic on the river was heavier. A telegraph (radio) station had been installed. But, above all, there were radios—battery-powered and electric-powered—which brought daily news of the outside world. The peasants of Itá, both in town and in the rural communities, were able to follow national political events and, more important to them, the progress of the international soccer games in Santiago, Chile, where Brazil again won the world championship. They knew about satellites. The new awareness of the outside world was illustrated dramatically by a barely literate Itá peasant. As he conversed with the author, while his wife squeezed *assái* (palm nut) juice with her hands, he asked if the satellite that could be seen in the skies every evening was "Russo" or "Americano."

But Itá is still isolated in comparison to other town-peasant communities. In other parts of Brazil, and in Latin America as a whole, such communities are more often found on motor roads than on rivers. In these localities, truck and bus drivers have become agents of change, transmitting outside influences from village to village and from the town to the countryside. In a few hours peasants now cover distances by motorcar that would have taken them days by donkey or on foot in the

recent past. Furthermore, outsiders including traders, missionaries, politicians, and others, now come to them with greater
frequency. Rural peasants can migrate to a distant city and
return. The total effect has been for the isolation of the town-
peasant community to break down, and its inhabitants, more
than ever before, to become members of regional and national
societies.

Despite the shortage of land adjacent to the town, the agriculturalists of Itá do not suffer from a chronic peasant ill,
namely *minifundio*. In much of Latin America Indian and
mestizo peasant landholdings have been subdivided by sale or
inheritance until they are below the minimum size sufficient to
provide a living for a family. "In Guatemala," Thomas F. Carroll estimates, "97 per cent of all farms are less than 20 hectares.* The corresponding figure for Peru and Ecuador is 90
per cent; for the Dominican Republic, it is 95 per cent; for
Venezuela, 88 per cent, and for the private sector of the Mexican farm economy, 88 per cent. In Colombia some 325,000
farms average 2½ hectares." (Carroll 1961:61.) In all these
countries the land shortage of the peasant is aggravated by the
presence of large commercial holdings—fincas, haciendas,
fazendas, or whatever they may be called. Even in Brazil,
with its immense territory, many peasant groups suffer from
land shortage and from the pressure of latifundios.†

Where peasants suffer from the extreme parcelization of
land and from lack of land resulting from the pressure of large
commercial holdings, land provides the basis for tension and

* One hectare is two and a half acres.
† According to the Brazilian census, 34.4 per cent of all agricultural
establishments was composed of tracts of less than ten hectares and altogether accounted for but 1.3 per cent of the land in cultivation. Another
51 per cent of all agricultural establishments was composed of tracts of
between ten and 100 hectares accounting for 15.3 per cent of the total
area. The remaining 14.6 per cent of agricultural holdings accounted for
83.4 per cent of the area.

even violence. Northeastern Brazil, the Cochabamba region of
Bolivia (Patch 1960:119 ff.), and highland Peru * are among
the best-known current examples of regions of peasant unrest
resulting mainly from land problems. In some cases, this unrest
has taken the form of forceful invasions of large plantations or
forceful resistance to eviction. Mainly as a reaction to land
problems, peasant leaders have appeared, and peasant organizations, such as the rapidly growing Peasant Leagues of northeastern Brazil and the campesino "syndicate" (*sindicato*) in
the department of Cochabamba in Bolivia, have taken form.
Although not unknown among Indian peasants, such peasant
leaders and organizations are more common among mestizos.
With more frequent relations with the outside and greater
awareness of regional and national issues, mestizo peasants are
becoming an increasingly articulate sector of Latin American
society. Even more than the Indians, they are at least potentially a focus of widespread social and political change.

THE PEASANTRY AND THE NATION: A CONCLUSION

Two types of Latin American Peasantry have been described, and each must be considered separately in terms of its
relationship to the nation of which it is a part. The Indian
peasant remains outside the nation in many ways, although
often remains outside the nation in many ways, although often
providing a necessary labor force for the national economy.
Indian peasants tend to be conservative, are sometimes resistant to change, and value continuity of their traditional forms.
They are not eager to exchange their community world view,
their own prestige system, and their separate identity for a
place on the lowest rung of the ladder of the national, social,

---

* At the symposium where this paper was read, Henry Dobyns reported that of 15 cases of violence in rural Peru, one case involved an
inter-indigenous land feud and most of the others involved police intervention to protect the land ownership system (haciendas).

and economic system.* Nevertheless, there is a marked trend throughout the highland Latin American countries, where Indian peasants still form a significant segment of the national population, for them to become mestizos, plantation laborers, or members of the urban poor. This process is stimulated by internal changes within the Indian peasant groups themselves, but just as often they are forced to migrate by the lack of land and the absence of other economic opportunities. Efforts to retain and to reform the Indian corporate community may delay the process for a time, but eventually Latin American countries will cease to be pluralistic or dualistic societies divided by Indians and mestizos (or ladinos, cholos, and other nationals). In time, all the population groups in these countries will fully identify themselves as members of a national system.

Everywhere in Latin America the mestizo peasants are more open to social change than the Indian peasants. They are often economically as badly off as the Indian peasants, but they have linguistic and cultural advantages. They speak the same language and they share the same ideal patterns of behavior as the middle-class and upper-class townspeople and urbanites of their nations, although their accent, grammar, and actual behavior may seem comical to their more sophisticated coun-

* Wolf, describing Mexican Indian Communities, has explained this conservatism in economic and functional terms. He wrote, "Lacking adequate resources in land, water, technical knowledge, and contacts in the market, the majority also lack the instruments which can transform into marketable commodities. At the same time, their inability to speak Spanish and their failure to understand the cues for the new patterns of nation-oriented behavior isolate them from the channels of communication between community and nation. Under these circumstances they must cling to the traditional "rejection pattern" of their ancestors, because their economic base sets limits to the introduction of new cultural alternatives. These are all too often nonfunctional for them. The production of sufficient maize for subsistence purposes remains their major goal in life. In their case the granting of ejidos tends to lend support to their accustomed way of life and reinforce their attachment to their traditional heritage." (1956:1073.)

trymen. Mestizo peasants are more apt to have higher material and educational aspirations, and are thus more vulnerable to political ideology than are Indian peasants. Because they have aspirations they cannot afford, they are more often frustrated than their Indian counterparts. They are thus more sensitive to outside leadership, and more apt to develop their own leaders in protest against their low position in the national society.

Both Indian and mestizo peasants are now, more than ever before, influenced by the national society.* In most Indian peasant villages, and certainly in all small towns where Indian and mestizo live together, there are individuals who may be described as cultural "brokers," to use Eric Wolf's term. In all small peasant communities, Indian, mestizo, or mixed, there are "individuals who are able to operate both in terms of community-orientation and national-oriented expectations. . . . They become the economic and political 'brokers' of nation-community relations, a function which carries its own rewards" (Wolf 1956b:1072.) These people derive their power from a simultaneous understanding of the local culture and of the national culture; they are a bridge, so to speak, to the outside. As Wolf states it, "They stand guard over the crucial junctures or synapse of relationships which connect the local system to the larger whole" (1956b:1075). They are individuals who know how to manipulate personal and traditional ties in the peasant village, but who also know how to translate these ties into a different kind of power on the outside.

Who are these cultural brokers? As yet, little is known about this important group, or better, these individuals, for it appears

* The concept of the "cultural broker" and the importance of the relationship of peasant communities to the larger society were pointed out during the discussion of an earlier draft of this paper by Manning Nash. Neither Nash nor the other participants are, of course, responsible for my own treatment of the "cultural broker" in these pages, which is meant to suggest important lines of future research.

that they usually operate as individuals. To date, most sociologists and anthropologists who have studied Latin American peasant societies have concentrated on the internal structure of the local community, rather than on the relationship of the local community to the larger society. Tentatively, however, it would seem obvious that such individuals fall into two general types, which might be called "traditional brokers" and "new brokers." The traditional broker is an individual whose role derives from traditional and internal relationships within the peasant community, whereas the new broker's role relates to the larger society and the new influences from the outside upon the local community.

Traditionally, of course, the broker was a *patrón*. He was the local trader upon whom the peasant depended for credit. In many Indian peasant communities, these brokers were the recruiters for work on coffee fincas (Guatemala) and coastal sugar plantations (Peru), and for work in the United States (Mexican braceros). In many peasant communities the local Padre was a traditional cultural broker, although the shortage of clergymen throughout Latin America meant that few Indian peasant communities had a resident priest. In mestizo peasant communities and in communities in which both Indians and mestizos lived, he was most often the local upper-class politician whose power depended almost entirely upon his role as a broker. Whoever he was, the traditional broker maintained his position through traditional roles—through his family, extended kinsmen, and compadres; through favors extended to the members of the community; and through an intimate knowledge of the local social scene and custom. His relationship with the community always had an element of noblesse oblige; he depended on tradition and established economic relations with the larger society for his position. The traditional broker is an influence for continuity, not for change.

The new cultural broker works generally for change. Some new cultural brokers are native sons of the community in which they live, and thus are fully aware of the traditional values and of the local social system. But even these native sons have lived in and learned something of the larger society, and they have accepted the values of the outside world. Throughout highland Latin America, there are a growing number of bilingual Indians who have spent considerable time on plantations and in large cities, and who have returned to live in their native communities. Many of them reject what they saw and learned while away from home, and attempt to reintegrate themselves into the local community. Others become innovators and cultural brokers. They have learned of the power of labor unions, political parties, and the judicial process. The young Indian political leaders who appeared in so many Guatemalan communities after the revolution of 1944 are good examples. *

Among mestizo peasants cultural brokers originating in the community are, of course, more numerous, since there is a greater awareness of the outside world and no linguistic barrier. Yet it would seem probable that few potential cultural brokers, with experience outside their local communities, actually return to perform that role in mestizo communities. The mestizo peasant community lacks the distinctive set of values and integration that encourages so many Indians to return.

* Juan Pérez Jolote, the Tzotzil-speaking Indian from Chamula in Chiapas, Mexico, whose story is told so vividly by Ricardo Pozas, is an example of an Indian who seems to have rejected his outside experience and to have reintegrated his life into the traditional community. (See Pozas 1962.) José Rojas, a Quechua-speaking peasant from the community of Ucurena in Cochabamba department of Bolivia, is an example of a man who became a native leader on his return. After living in Argentina, Rojas returned to Ucurena where "he worked as a laborer while he assisted in organizing the *campesinas.*" He ultimately became a national figure as campesino leader. (See Patch 1960:119–20.)

Mestizo peasants, already consciously a part of the larger society, are more apt than Indians never to return home, especially if they are successful in the larger society. Like the United States, every village and small town in Latin America has its native sons who were successful in the city and never returned. But a few individuals do return, and they are important in interpreting the outside society to their compatriots.

Finally, one must consider the new cultural brokers who come from outside the local community. As national institutions penetrate peasant communities, they bring cultural brokers from the outside—teachers, agronomists, public health officers, Peace Corps personnel, Protestant and Catholic missionaries, and politicians. Most of these people cannot fulfill the role of a cultural broker, for they do not understand the local society in which they are assigned to work. But, increasingly, they are being taught to be cultural brokers—by UNESCO in its school at Patzcuaro, by the Peace Corps, and by Latin American governments, which realize the great gulf that exists between technically trained personnel from the cities and the mass of people with whom they must work. Important among the new brokers from outside the community are, of course, politicians, labor leaders, and others who are consciously attempting to awaken political consciousness among peasant groups. More and more, politicians find the peasants ready to listen and to participate. Often the peasants do not fully understand the leaders from the outside, and, in many countries where literacy is a requirement for voting, they have no recourse to the polls. The time may not be too far off, however, when nationally organized peasant groups will wield decisive political power in many nations of Latin America. Already in several Latin American nations, such as Venezuela, Colombia, Bolivia, and Mexico, the peasant is considered an important locus of political power. Crucial to the form and direction that such political movements will take are the people we have called the new cultural brokers.

The sources of change for the peasant community of Latin America must come from the larger society of which it is now a part. Change will probably originate in the political process, and economic change will follow. Land reform, technical assistance, credit, and education for the peasant will be part of the platform of political parties seeking their support. Such change may be slow, unequal, and painful, but it would seem to be inevitable if Latin American societies are to enter the modern world. Latin American nations cannot continue with a large segment of their people neglected, impoverished, illiterate, and living in isolation inside their frontiers. The peasants may not be the wave of the future in Latin America, but certainly they are the material—the human mass—out of which the future will be made.

[V]

THE CONCEPT OF SOCIAL RACE
IN THE AMERICAS

THE present paper is concerned with a limited aspect of race
relations in the Americas, namely, with the systems of classification of people into "social races" that have been used in the
past and are used today in our American societies. The term
"social race" is used because these groups or categories are
socially, not biologically, defined in all of our American societies, although the terms by which they are labeled may have
originally referred to biological characteristics (Wagley 1952:
14). Such terms as "Negro," "white," "Indian," or "mulatto" do
not have genetic meanings in most of our American societies:
in one society they may be classifications based on real or
imaginary physical characteristics; in another they may refer
more to criteria of social status such as education, wealth, language, and custom; while in still another they may indicate
near or distant ancestry. Thus the same man might be classed
as a mulatto in Brazil, a Negro in the United States, and perhaps a mestizo in Mexico. In this paper, the point of view is
taken that the way people are classified in social races in a
multiracial society tells us much about the relations between

This paper was written in 1957 while in residence at the Center for
Advanced Study in the Behavioral Sciences. It was originally published
in the *Actas del XXXIII Congress Internacional de Americanistas* (Tomo
I, pp. 403–417), 1959, San José, Costa Rica.

such groups. More specifically, the criteria for defining social races differs from region to region in the Americas. In one region *ancestry* is stressed, in another region *sociocultural* criteria are emphasized, and in still another, *physical appearance* is the primary basis for classifying people according to social race. This produces in each of these regions a different number of social races and different structural arrangements for race relations. The different ways in which each region conceives social races reflect the relations between people of diverse biological and cultural origin within a larger society.

An understanding of how these different classifications of social race came about and of the different functions they have played in the various nations can be gained by looking at some of the simple and relatively well-known facts regarding the formation of the populations of our American nations. All of our American nations are multiracial in some degree. Biologically speaking the population of the New World has been formed by three racial stocks—the Amerindian of Mongoloid derivation, the African Negroid, and the European Caucasoid. Each of these three racial stocks has made contributions in different proportions in the various regions of the Americas. Amerindians predominated in the highland countries from Mexico south of Chile; Negroes formed numerically the most important element of the population in the lowland region from southern United States, into the Caribbean, and on the South American mainland south into Brazil; Caucasoids have contributed in greatest numbers in the northern and southern most extremes of our continents—namely, in Canada and northern United States and in Uruguay, Argentina, and Chile. Yet everywhere the three racial stocks have each contributed in some degree to the contemporary populations.

Likewise, throughout the Americas, the process of intermixture between the three racial stocks began early—almost at once after the arrival of the Europeans and their African slaves in the New World. In the highland countries, the Spanish conquistadors mated freely with Indian women, and by the end of the sixteenth century people of mixed Spanish-Indian ancestry were relatively numerous throughout the highland countries. Furthermore, in Mexico and also in other highland countries, a considerable number of African slaves were imported to work in the mines and on the plantations—the majority of these Africans were males and they too mated with Indian women. Their offspring added to the racially mixed population and further complicated the types of mixtures present in colonial society.

In the tropical and semitropical regions of the Americas, a similar process of race mixture began soon after 1500. At first the Spanish, Portuguese, and English mated with Indian women. But since the Indian population was sparse compared to the highlands, and since many tribes were soon decimated as a result of contact with Europeans, such unions were not numerous and did not produce a large European-Indian mixed population as they did in the highlands. Nevertheless, in certain areas of the lowlands European-Indian populations were important; in Brazil, the *mamelucos*—children of Portuguese fathers and Indian mothers—became relatively numerous in the late sixteenth century, and in Paraguay where the Spanish conquistadors lived as the owners of veritable harems of Indian women, a mixed European-Indian group soon became the most important element of the colonial population. But, throughout most of the tropical lowland region, the formation of a mixed population comparable to that in the highlands awaited the arrival of the flood of African slaves.

From the middle of the sixteenth century until the end of the eighteenth century, this region received literally millions of Negroes, mainly from West Africa. The story of miscegenation of the European slaveowners with their female slaves is so well known that it need not be documented here. Such unions were probably most frequent in Brazil and in the West Indies between Spanish, Portuguese, and French males and Negro women. This has been attributed, particularly in the case of the Portuguese, to a lack of prejudice—even considerable attraction—toward women of darker hues (Freyre 1964:4). But the men from these Latin countries were not alone in being attracted to Negro women. The Dutch and the English also mated frequently with Negroid women. Although the laws and social pressure against miscegenation were stronger in the English colonies (and later in the United States) than in the colonies of other European powers, there is no doubt that miscegenation was almost as frequent. This is attested by the large mulatto population which took form in the British Islands and in southern United States. By 1850, for example, about one-twelfth of the slave population of the United States and over a third of the "free" Negroes were said to be of mixed Negro-Caucasoid ancestry (Frazier 1949:67).

Miscegenation took place also on a large scale even in those regions which are today predominantly European. In Canada during the eighteenth and early nineteenth century, the so-called *métis*—the offspring of French fur traders and Indian women—outnumbered Europeans in western Canada. In Argentina, mestizos (Indian-Europeans) greatly outnumbered people of European ancestry until after the middle of the nineteenth century. In both Uruguay and Argentina, there was an appreciable number of mulattoes and Negroes during the first half of the eighteenth century.* There have been numerous explanations for the disappearance of these people of Negroid

* According to the estimate of the Argentine sociologist Ingenieros (cited in Taylor 1948:56), in 1869 the Argentine population contained: 350,000 whites; 1,315,000 mestizos; 120,000 mulattoes; 3,000 Indians; and 15,000 Negroes. It was essentially a mixed population.

ancestry and of the large number of mestizos in Argentina and Uruguay; an example is the explanation that they were killed off in the various wars (Vidart 1955:57). But it should be obvious that they were almost totally physically assimilated by the great wave of European immigrants of the late nineteenth and early twentieth centuries.

Throughout the Americas the process of miscegenation between Caucasoids, Amerindians, and Negroes produced hybrid populations. It also produced a complicated social hierarchy in which racial appearance or ancestry was perhaps the most important criterion of rank. At first this social-racial hierarchy was simple. Everywhere the European whites dominated the American Indians and African slaves by force. In the social hierarchy the European whites were on top, and the Indians and Africans were on the bottom. Caucasoid physical features were symbolic of membership in the "superior" social group, and Amerindian and Negroid physical features were symbolic of membership in the "inferior" groups. But within a generation the process of miscegenation produced intermediate groups who were intermediate not only in their physical appearance but also in social status. During the early colonial period, it was usual to attempt to describe such people in terms of their mixed ancestry, their intermediate physical appearance, and their intermediate social position. In order to account for these groups of mixed ancestry and the intermediate social status accruing to them, it was necessary to develop a profusion of categories of social race, especially in those regions where intermixture of the component racial stocks was greatest.

In Brazil, in addition to the *brancos* (whites), *Indios* or *Indígenas* (Indians), and *pretos*, there were mamelucos (Indian-Portuguese), mulattoes (Portuguese-Negro), *cafusos* (Negro-Indian), *cabras* (Portuguese-mulatto), as well as terms for other mixtures (Ramos 1944:205). For Mexico, Aguirre Beltrán has brought together a series of systems of classification of social race or, in other terms, the system of *castas* that took form in the seventeenth century; in each of these systems a long series of ancestral types and degrees of intermixture, each with its relative position in accordance with "closeness" to full Spanish ancestry, are listed. In one system described by Aguirre Beltrán (1940:166–72), in addition to *bermejos* (that is, whites or Spaniards) and *indios* (Indians), there are: *negros* (Negroes), divided into two categories; mulattoes, divided into seven categories; and mestizos, divided into five categories. Although these were color categories, they were also based on other anatomical characteristics such as hair, lips, and nose. Ancestry was often specified; a *mulato morisco,* for example, was specifically "the offspring of a Spaniard and a *mulata*" (Aguirre Beltrán 1940:167). Likewise, throughout the Caribbean region there was a proliferation of social racial categories based primarily on skin color but also ancestry. Perhaps the most elaborate of these is the system ascribed to Haiti in the eighteenth century by Moreau de Saint Mery (1797, Tome I:68–88). Saint Mery explained the system by attributing 128 parts (almost like genes) to all men. A *blanc* (white) has 128 parts white, a *Négre* (Negro) 128 parts black, and the offspring—a *mulâtre* (mulatto)—64 parts white and 64 parts black. In addition he listed *sacatra* (8 to 23 parts white); *griffe* (24 to 39 parts white); *marabou* (40 to 48) *quateron* (71 to 100); *métif* (101 to 112) *mamelouc* (113 to 120) *quateronné* (121 to 124) and finally a *sang-mêlé* (125 to 127). (Saint Mery 1797, Tome I:86.)

Even within the southern United States, the slaves were often differentiated according to ancestral types such as mulatto, quadroon (one-quarter Negro ancestry), octaroon (one-eighth Negro ancestry), and mustie (near white). Although still slaves, these people of intermediate ancestry were considered by their owners to be more intelligent, they brought higher prices in the slave market, and they received preferred occupations on the plantations. Furthermore, they were more often freed (sometimes by their white fathers), and the "free Negroes," who were relatively numerous, especially in Charleston and in New Orleans, were mainly of mixed ancestry (Frazier 1949:76 ff.).*

Everywhere in the Americas these early systems of classification of people emphasized ancestry as well as physical appearance as their dominant criteria. They also represented a preoccupation with the intermediate social position of such groups between the dominant Caucasoids and the Negro slaves and the subjugated American Indians. But for several reasons, such elaborate systems of classification soon became unworkable and impossible to maintain. First, they could not possibly be extended in complexity to account for all possible mixtures. As mating took place not only between whites, Indians, and Negroes but also between individuals of the growing variety of race mixtures, the number of categories theoretically had to be amplified. One system for Mexico reported the type called *Ahi-te-Estas*, an illustration of the absurd lengths to which such classifications could be extended. The Ahi-te-Estas was a person born of one *coyote-mestizo* and one mulatto parent. A coyote-mestizo, in turn, was a person born of one *chamizo* and one Indian parent, and a chamizo was the offspring of one

* Aguirre Beltrán gives examples of a series of "erudite" classifications which were set down in the early nineteenth century in New Spain which are as complex as that given by Moreau de Saint Mery. According to Aguirre Beltrán, these systems "fortunately never were carried into practice" (1940:175). Like the "theoretical" system of Moreau de Saint Mery, they do, however, indicate the growing complexity of attempting to take into account the various types of intermixtures.

coyote and one mulatto (Whetten 1948:51–52). Obviously, as mixing between the various types continued, such systems became even theoretically impossible to maintain.

Second, although most of the systems described ancestry, they also implied either explicitly or implicitly that individuals of a given category would probably share a similar phenotypical appearance; that is, a person who was a mulatta of one white and one Negro parent would have a physical type intermediate between Caucasoid and Negroid. This was roughly so as long as it involved mating between individuals of two distinct racial stocks. But as soon as the situation involved the mating between the intermediate types themselves, physical appearance no longer was so indicative of ancestry. Not all individuals—including offspring of the same parents, who had three white ancestors and one Negro ancestor, for example—had a similar phenotype. The genetic process of transmission of physical characteristics does not work like the combination of chemical elements. Rather the genes of the parents sort themselves out quite distinctly in the different progeny. It was perfectly possible, therefore, to have two individuals both of whom were by the criterion of ancestry moriscos (that is, one Spanish and one mulatto parent according to the same complex scheme mentioned above for Mexico), but who by the criterion of physical appearance could be placed in different categories. If one child were dark in skin color, he would be a mulatto (one Spanish and one mulatto parent); the child lighter in skin color might be an *albino* (one Spanish and one morisco).

But perhaps the most important reason that such complex schemes were destined to fall out of use was the fact that sociocultural criteria were not only implied by a term for a category but soon came into play in placing an individual in such groups. In the sixteenth century, the terms *gaupuchin, criollo,* Negro, and Indian in Mexico described with relative certainly not only a physical type but also the occupation, wealth, education, and language of a group. Similarly *preto* (Negro) in Brazil in the early period implied slave status and *branco* the status of a free man. But throughout the Americas, in greater or lesser degree, a conflict began to develop between classification of an individual by either ancestry or physical appearance and these social and cultural criteria. Soon there was the anomaly of those individuals who were Indians and mestizos in terms of ancestry and physical appearance but who were Spanish "whites" in terms of language, dress, education, wealth, and other social and cultural characteristics. Or there were free people of Negroid ancestry and physical appearance who by sociocultural criteria should be mulattoes or even whites. Clearly a Spanish-speaking individual who was wealthy could not be classed with the people living in an isolated and primitive village despite his Amerindian physical appearance and ancestry; similarly a black professor could not be classed with the black workers on a plantation. Social and cultural criteria became entangled with criteria of ancestry and phenotypical appearance, further complicating and confusing these systems of classifying people by social race.

During the nineteenth century, partially as a reaction to the idealistic creeds of the new American republics, there was a widespread trend to resolve this conflict between the classification of people simultaneously by physical appearance, ancestry, and sociocultural status. The conflict became especially acute with the abolition of slavery in those regions with a large slave population and as social and economic mobility increased the number of people who were Negro, mulatto, Indian, mestizo, or other intermediate types in physical appearance but "white" in accordance with social and cultural status. Everywhere there seems to have been a simplification of the systems of classification of people by social race. Numerous intermediate types based primarily on ancestry and color disappeared from official usage, but not entirely from the popular vocabulary in many regions and countries. In Spanish America all of the intermediate types of the so-called "castas" fell out of general use and such broad categories as mestizo, ladino, and cholo came to be used. In Brazil, at least such terms as *pardo* (literally "brown") and *caboclo* (meaning any lower class rural person of mixed ancestry) supplanted the more elaborate terms once used for intermediate types. In the United States although mulatto was used on several occasions as a category in taking the census, the terms for various degrees of Negro-white ancestry disappeared from general usage.

But more important a basic difference, perhaps already apparent in the earlier periods, appeared between the different regions and countries in the Americas as to the criteria used in classifying people by social race. And this difference in criteria has continued into the twentieth century to set the frame of reference for race relations in the different regions. This difference consists of making use of, or placing greater weight upon, one of the three sets of criteria for classification mentioned above, namely, *ancestry, physical appearance,* and *sociocultural status.*

Broadly speaking the United States stands apart from most of Latin America in making use of ancestry almost exclusively in defining who is Negro and who is white. Curiously, during slavery more weight was given to social and cultural criteria; despite the fact that many slaves were of obvious mixed ancestry; it was their legal condition that placed them in a slave category. And during slavery a relatively large number of free people of color stressed their intermediate brown color and their intermediate social position between the slaves and the whites. But by the late nineteenth century there was a decided shift in the criteria used to classify people as to social race, and the possibility of a social race of mulattoes, intermediate in physical appearance and social position, was precluded. The dominant whites were able to establish a rule of descent based on ancestry which stated that anyone who had a known Negro ancestor was a Negro. This rule became a law in many southern states. Thus the system of classification of people by social race was reduced to a twofold caste-like system of "Negroes" and "whites." Not even the fair skinned individual with Caucasoid features with a remote Negro ancestor can be classed as a "white," although thoroughly adapted in occupation, education, social graces, and economic position to middle or upper class status. This did not prevent a large number of such people, however, from "passing" as white (that is, assuming the status of a white by migrating to a locality where one's ancestry is unknown); and it did not prevent the Negroes themselves from making use of the other criteria of physical appearance and social and cultural status in determining rank within their own caste.

The formation of this system of two caste-like social races was of course the reflection of, and a result of, the pattern of relations between Negroes and whites that took form after abolition. It provided a structure favorable to a system of segregation. With but two groups vis-à-vis each other, segregation in schools, housing, public conveyances, restaurants, and other public meeting places was feasible. The difficulties of segregation under another system of classification of people by social race is brought home strikingly when we allow ourselves to imagine the complexities of segregation in the United States if the intermediate position of mulattoes, quadroons, and octaroons was recognized today. If segregation on the basis of but two social races is considered costly to the nation, then it would have been prohibitive to provide "parallel" facilities for four or five separate social races. In the United States, by emphasizing ancestry combined with a rule of descent, a system of two caste-like social races with little mobility between the groups has been amenable to segregation and productive of tension.

In the region of the Americas which consists of Mexico and Guatemala (and this probably also applies to Ecuador, Peru, and Bolivia which have large Indian populations), the classification of people by social race took another form in the nineteenth and twentieth centuries. In this region the emphasis has been placed mainly on the criteria of social and cultural status, almost to the point of ignoring the criterion of physical appearance. Furthermore, except within certain local communities, ancestry as a criterion for membership in a social race has little or no importance. In each of these countries there continues to be a relatively large segment of the population classified as "indígenas" or Indians, an intermediate social race called mestizo in Mexico and ladino in Guatemala, and finally a social race which we might call the whites. The difficulty in distinguishing between Indian and mestizo (or ladino) on any basis except social and cultural criteria such as language, custom, community membership, costume, and self-identification is well known and need not be restated here. It is enough to say that physical appearance seldom serves as a criterion on which to classify a person in one of these two groups. Similarly, although a highly educated man in the city might have Indian-mestizo physical features, it would be difficult to classify him as mestizo or ladino. The answer to this lack of emphasis upon physical appearance as a criterion for classifying individuals as to social race is that there is an almost imperceptible gradation of physical appearance from Amerindian to Caucasoid running from the Indians to the whites. This is the result, of course, of a high frequency of miscegenation be-tween Indians and Europeans in the colonial period and, as we shall see, from continued biological intermixture even today.

Yet something must be said concerning the importance given to ancestry as a criterion for social racial classification in Mexico and Guatemala. It is probably true that in these coun-tries (and in the other Indian countries) ancestry is still an important criterion for membership in the group of "aristo-cratic families" who claim "pure" European descent, sometimes conveniently forgetting an Indian ancestor in colonial times. Yet such aristocratic families form but a small segment of the whites. But ancestry as a criterion is also important in some regions of Mexico and Guatemala where in local communities it is applied with a force that is reminiscent of the United States. In the region of southeastern Guatemala, in the north-western highlands of the same country, in highland Chiapas, and perhaps in other local regions where relations between Indians and non-Indians are tense, it is virtually impossible for an Indian to overcome *within his own community* the criterion of ancestry and to become a mestizo or ladino on the basis of social and cultural criteria. This creates a twofold caste-like situation similar to that in the United States (Tumin 1952; Gillin 1951). But there is a vast difference between the two situations. Lacking emphasis on physical appearance as a cri-terion for social race, it is easier to "pass"; and it is always possible for an Indian who leaves his home community and who acquires the social and cultural criteria of a mestizo or ladino to lose his identification as an Indian and to be accepted as a ladino or mestizo. Furthermore, the emphasis on ancestry pro-ducing a caste-like structure is far from universal within these nations. In other regions of Guatemala, for example, it is pos-sible for the offspring of a man of known Indian ancestry who acquires ladino culture to be classed as a ladino; and in Mexico, Beals speaks of whole Tarascan communities which "may gradually shift through time from being Indian to being regarded as mestizo" (Beals 1955:422). There can be no clearer witness to the emphasis on sociocultural criteria to the almost total exclusion of the criteria of both physical appearance and ancestry than the fact that *a whole community can change its social race presumably without a change in physical type.*

Like the caste-like system of the United States, the system of social race of Mexico and Guatemala reflects the kind of relationship that has taken form between the various groups. Indians are looked down on and discriminated against by non-Indians. But contrary to the situation of the Negro in the United States, they are not being identified by the indelible criterion of physical appearance nor are they placed in the "inferior" group by ancestry. There is then a greater possibility for individual, and even whole community, mobility from Indian to mestizo. Furthermore, while the system of social race of the United States actually perpetuates itself, the system of Mexico and Guatemala seems to contain in itself the seeds of its own destruction. Miscegenation between Negro and white in the United States only adds to the numbers of the Negro group. In Mexico intermarriage between Indian and mestizo, mestizo and white, or Indian and white generally adds to the mestizo group. The offspring of such unions are usually raised within the mestizo culture and thus become mestizos. And this system promotes continued racial intermixture; an individual who is an Indian in physical appearance but classed as a mestizo on the basis of social and cultural criteria will most probably mate with a mestizo, and raise his or her offspring as such. Theoretically, it is only a question of time until such populations may be entirely classed as mestizo by social race, and social differentiation will be entirely in terms of socio-economic classes.

Finally, in Brazil and in the Caribbean region of the Americas, the system of classification of people by social race has taken still another turn. In this region emphasis has been placed on physical appearance rather than on ancestry or social and cultural criteria.* In this region of the Americas there are no striking cultural contrasts comparable to those between Indians and non-Indians in Mexico and Guatemala. There are religious beliefs and rituals of African origin in some localities such as Haiti and northern Brazil. And, in some parts of the Caribbean a creole language, partially derived from Africa, is spoken by peasants. These cultural and linguistic traits are often identified with the Negro, but they are hardly limited to those classed as Negroes, for they are shared by a wide variety of people regardless of social race. The criterion of ancestry seems to be important in the Caribbean and Brazil —as it is in Mexico and Guatemala—only among those segments of the population who seek to prove the purity of their European—derived lineage. For the large mass of people, ancestry seldom acts to place an individual in a particular social race. But the indelible marks of physical appearance, with the highest prestige accruing to Caucasoid features and the lowest to Negroid features, remain important as criteria by which to classify people in social races. Throughout this whole region features such as color, the shape of the lips, hair texture, and

* In two brilliant essays (1959a and 1959b) the Brazilian sociologist Oracy Nogueira has examined the different consequences between "prejudice of color" ("*marca*" or "*côr*") in Brazil and "prejudice of origin" in the United States. In my terms, this distinction is between the criteria of physical appearance (Brazil and the Caribbean) and ancestry (United States). I have drawn heavily on these two essays but I have attempted to stress the structural consequences of the use of these different criteria rather than their consequences in the type of prejudice, as did Nogueira.

the shape of the nose are closely analyzed in order to place an individual in the proper social race.

But in populations such as those of Brazil and the Caribbean where mixture between the racial stocks had been so extensive, there is a tremendous variety in physical appearance. Although such terms as mulatto, "people of color," and pardo (brown) are used to describe a wide range of physical types intermediate between Negro and white, in popular usage there are many more precise terms describing people of intermediate social races. For example in one Brazilian community with a highly variegated population, Hutchinson lists eight categories and several subcategories descriptive of people of Negro and mixed Negro-white descent. In this one community individuals are classified as: (1) *preto,* Negro or dark black; (2) *cabra* (female *cabrocha*), lighter in skin color than *preto,* hair less kinky, and facial features less Negroid; (3) *cabo verde,* dark skin color but straight hair, thin lips, and narrow nose; (4) *escuro,* literally a dark man but meaning dark skin with some Caucasoid features—most often used for an individual who does not quite fit the three categories above; (5) *mulato,* yellowish skin color, kinky to curly hair, thin to thick lips, narrow to wide nose—subtypes are light and dark mulatto; (6) *pardo,* a classification most often used officially for census and the like, but sometimes applied in common parlance for individuals who "are closer to the white than a light mulatto"; (7) *sarará,* light skin, reddish blond but kinky hair, and Negroid facial features; and (8) *moreno,* literally brunette—"excellent" fair skin, dark curly hair, features . . . much more Caucasoid than Negroid." (Hutchinson 1957:120.) Similar systems of multiple categories have been reported for other Brazilian communities by Harris (1956:119ff.), Nogueira (1955:460), Pierson (1942:135–36), Zimmerman (1952) and Wagley (1953). Although none have as many category-terms as that described by Hutchinson, all contain from four to seven category-terms.*

Likewise, the societies of the Caribbean are characterized by the classification of people by a series of terms describing their social racial appearance and again, as in Brazil, such features as skin color, nose, lips, and hair textures are the diagnostic traits. In the French West Indies, for example, there are such terms as *béké* (white), *mulâtre clair* (or blanc), *mulâtre foncé* or *noir* (dark or black mulatto), *câpre* (straight hair but mulatto or Negroid features), *chabin* (rather dark skin but Caucasoid features and light-colored hair), *négre* (Negro), and *congo* (very black with "bad" features) (Leiris 1955). Similar systems of multiple categories of social race are reported by Henriques (1953) for Jamaica, by Steward and associates (1956) for Puerto Rico, and by Crowley (1957) for Trinidad, to cite but three examples.

What is distinctive about these Brazilian and Caribbean systems of social race is that they are actually a continuum from Caucasoid through the various degrees of mixed physical appearance to Negroid. They do not in themselves form social groups that interact vis-à-vis one another as do Indian and mestizo in Mexico, and Negro and white in the United States. They are a way of describing and classifying individuals according to physical appearance, but this is just one way that these societies classify people. The position of an individual in the hierarchy of social race combined with education, economic status, occupation, family connnections, even manners and artistic abilities places one in his or her proper rank. Each of the categories of social race is divided by socioeconomic classes, although it must be said that the largest proportion of Negroes is in the lower classes and the majority of the upper

* In a later study of a small fishing village in Bahia State, forty terms descriptive of racial types were recorded (Harris 1964; Kottak 1965).

class is white since educational and economic opportunities for mobility have not been generalized. Neither Negroes, mulattoes, pardos, whites, nor any other social race acts as a group or attempts to improve their situation as a group. Therefore this situation is less conducive to discrimination and segregation on the basis of social race. Yet given the presence of relatively rigid socioeconomic classes deriving from the colonial period, class discrimination and segregation often function in a manner superficially similar to racial discrimination and segregation.

In addition these Brazilian and Caribbean systems of social race provide a situation favorable to individual mobility. An individual does not "pass" from Indian to mestizo nor from Negro to white. Rather by means of improving his education, financial position, and other qualities capable of modification within a lifetime, he may move up in the class structure while still remaining "low" in the hierarchy of social race. People politely try to ignore such an individual's disability of personal appearance. There is then a noted tendency in such societies to "lighten the skin" of individuals who have other qualifications for high rank, except for personal appearance or social race. Thus a man who is dark in skin color and who has Negroid features but who is a well-placed engineer or physician, for example, may be classed as a moreno or a pardo rather than as a dark mulatto or Negro. Even physical appearance is often perceived subjectively and distorted by other criteria. Only a sense of the ridiculous prevents Brazilians from literally enacting their traditional statement that "A rich Negro is a white man and a poor white man is a Negro;" in some degree this statement applies to the Caribbean as well.

Each of these systems of classifying people by social race produces a very different structural situation for race relations. Each defines social races in different terms. In Mexico and

Guatemala (and elsewhere in the Indian countries) an Indian is defined in sociocultural terms. In the United States, a Negro is defined in terms of ancestry alone. In the Caribbean and in Brazil, social racial types are defined on the basis of physical appearance as modified in their perception by the total social status of the individual. These different definitions of social race have different consequences and thus so-called "race problems" are different problems in each of the three regions. In the United States, the definition of the Negro in terms of ancestry has created two caste-like social races, and the race problem of the United States consists of the struggle of the Negroes as a group to achieve equality of opportunity vis-à-vis the whites. But even if equality of opportunity is achieved by the Negroes in the United States, the continued presence of the two self-perpetuating caste-like social races will provide a situation highly conducive to continued competition and conflict. In Mexico and Guatemala, it might be said that there are also two self-conscious groups—Indians and non-Indians—and that the Indians act to improve their position as a group vis-à-vis the non-Indians. Yet by defining Indian in cultural terms, the way is always left open for individuals and whole communities to transform themselves from Indians into non-Indians. In the Caribbean and in Brazil, the situation is highly permissive to individual mobility. Social races do not form self-conscious groups, and "race relations" do not take the form of interaction between "racial" groups. Despite low position in the hierarchy of social races, individuals can improve their total position in society by achievement in other ways. Yet rigid barriers of socioeconomic classes operate to reduce the mobility of all people of low socioeconomic status; the "race problem" of this region is to a large extent a problem of socioeconomic classes.

Yet in all of our American societies, classifications of social race, however defined, remain a basis for formal or informal social, economic, and even legal discrimination, and often these classifications are bases of prejudice against whole groups. In view of the extensive miscegenation between people of all three major racial stocks and between the various intermediate types, and especially in view of the criteria used to define these social races, it is clear that nowhere do such categories as mulatto, Negro, Indian, mestizo, and white have genetic validity. But in the course of our American experience such racial terms have become entangled with social and cultural meanings and they remain symbols out of the past of slavery, peonage, and cultural differences to plague a large segment of our American people.

[VI]

KINSHIP PATTERNS IN BRAZIL:
THE PERSISTENCE OF
A CULTURAL TRADITION

THE varieties of kinship systems in primitive societies and the role of kinship in channeling social norms and behavior have been favorite subjects of study on the part of social anthropologists for over a century. In primitive societies, the study of kinship is almost synonymous with the study of *society,* so important are the rights, obligations, and expected patterns of behavior that are determined by kinship. Until recently, however, sociologists and anthropologists have all but ignored the role of kinship in our more complex modern societies. There has been considerable interest in and research on the family, but comparatively little attention has been given to the wider network of kinship. In fact, we have tended to view our modern institutions as essentially antagonistic to extended kinship bonds and obligations. It has generally been assumed that the social changes set off by the Industrial Revolution universally tend to isolate the immediate family from their kindred.

In recent years, however, anthropologists and sociologists have begun to suspect that this trend is not inevitable. Garigue (1956:1090–1101), for example, found extensive kinship net-

This paper first appeared in a volume of essays in honor of Professor Frank Tannenbaum entitled *Politics of Change in Latin America,* edited by Joseph Maier and Richard W. Weatherhead (Praeger, 1964).

works playing an important role in the social life of the French
Canadians living in Montreal despite a high degree of urbanization and industrialization. Raymond Firth and his associates
(1956) found extended kinship ties important in the lives of
Italians living in London. And, to cite but one more example,
Young and Wilmott (1957:xvi) were "surprised to discover
that the wider family, far from having disappeared, was still
much alive in the middle of London." It becomes apparent,
then, that widely extended kinship ties are not entirely incom-
patible with our modern institutions and that kinship continues
to have an important role in certain areas of our modern Western world.

The importance of kinship in the Brazilian tradition is well
known. Gilberto Freyre in his now-classical studies (1936;
1943) has shown conclusively the importance of the patriarchal family in the development of Brazilian society. These
large and powerful patriarchal families are now, in the main, a
thing of the past. As the agrarian society of yesterday gave
way to the urban-oriented and more industrialized society of
today, the large patriarchal families became disorganized. As
one writer on the modern Brazilian family has stated, "The
extended patriarchal family as an integrated social unit no
longer exists" (Hutchinson, C.J.A. 1955:261–74). Still another
student of the Brazilian family today writes that "the family no
longer is an economic and political group, nor is it any longer
the all-important group in social organization" (Candido
1951). There can be no doubt that the patriarchal family
regime has come to an end; but this does not mean that kinship no longer has an important function in contemporary
Brazilian society.

It is the thesis of this paper that, while the patriarchal
family type of the agrarian past might have disappeared, a
larger network of relatives, which I shall call the *parentela*, has

persisted with modified but important functions in Brazilian social, economic, and even political life.

The Luso-Brazilian parentela, as I am using the term, means all those relatives traced on both maternal and paternal lines whom an individual recognizes as kinsmen. It also includes one's affinals as well as those individuals who are related by the ceremonial ties of the *compadrio*. I do not need to describe the system by which kinsmen of such parentelas are classified, for that system is shared by all European cultures. In this system of kinship, which is bilateral and includes both the matrilineal and patrilineal lines, literally hundreds of individuals may be considered relatives, as long as the genealogical connection can be remembered. In anthropological terms, the Brazilian parentela is a kindred.

The various community studies that have been carried out in Brazil during the last decade provide us with rich data on the role of the parentela in Brazilian society. Most of the communities studied have been small; often they have been relatively isolated; and, in general, they were located in the more conservative north of Brazil. They admittedly do not provide us with a picture of the way of life in large cities or in the extreme south, where the influence of Northern European immigrants has been felt so strongly. It might be said that, in the main, the community studies we now have at hand reveal "traditional" Brazilian culture, which is being modified in larger centers and in the more rapidly changing rural zones of the country. Still, they offer a rich source of empirical data covering several regions of the country and a variety of ecological adaptations.

What do some of these studies reveal regarding the parentela and its functions? Not all of them discuss the parentela explicitly. As is so often the case, the term "family" is frequently used in several ways. It is used to mean the nuclear

group of man, wife, and children; the household unit; a patriarchal extended family; and sometimes it refers to a large network of kin—the parentela. None of the authors of these community studies has made an exhaustive analysis of the
parentela and its functions. Perhaps because there is nothing
exotic or strange about the workings of our own Western kinship system, we have tended to overlook its importance in our
own social structure. Yet it seems clear from these community
studies that kinship has an important role in Brazilian social
relations.

There is neither time nor space to present all of the data
regarding the parentela from the numerous community studies
available to us from Brazil. In the pages that follow, however,
I have summarized the data for seven communities on which
data on the "family" has been published.*

VILA RECÔNCAVO (Hutchinson, H. W. 1957)

The community of Vila Recôncavo is situated on the Bay of
All Saints in the region known as the Recôncavo, just forty-one
kilometers for the city of Salvador in Bahia State. The Recôncavo is perhaps the oldest sugar-producing region in all of
Brazil, and sugar cane is still by far the most important economic pursuit in the region. (Petroleum is, however, now
being pumped from the sugar-cane fields.) The community of
Vila Recôncavo consists of a small town (a county seat) of
1,462 people and of the people living on the sugar-cane plantations and at the sugar factory in the rural zone. The inhabitants of the rural area number about 2,800, of whom 500 are
concentrated near the sugar factory while the rest live on the
sugar plantations. Hutchinson describes four social classes for

* The studies of Minas Velhas and Vila Recôncavo were part of the
program of community studies sponsored by Columbia University and
the State of Bahia and directed by Thales de Azevedo, of the University
of Bahia, and the author. The studies of Passagem Grande, Cerrado, and
Retiro were carried out under a similar program sponsored by the São
Francisco Valley Authority and directed by Donald Pierson.

Vila Recôncavo: Class A, an upper class of landowners who live on their plantations and spend part of each year in the city of Salvador; Class B, a middle class made up of local bureaucrats, merchants, and professional people who live in town, and plantation administrators, technicians, and specialists at the sugar factory and on plantations; Class C, a lower class of fishermen and artisans who live in the city and of mill workers and field hands in the rural zone; and Class D, a marginal lower class of servants, laundresses, and others lacking steady employment.

Many of the landowners in the Vila Recôncavo upper class are descendants of the *senhores de engenho* of the past, and they have clung to many of their aristocratic patterns of behavior. This class consists of "five family lines which own practically all of the sugar lands in the area" (Hutchinson, H.W. 1957: 127) and dominate the community politically and socially. "Two of these families . . . are closely interwoven by first-cousin marriage; a third . . . is related to these two by marriage" (Hutchinson, H.W. 1957:127). From the point of view of any member, these three families constitute one large parentela. Hutchinson (1957:128–35) reports only seventy-eight consangiuneous relatives among the two closely interwoven families in the community; but it must be remembered that these people divided their time between Vila Recôncavo and the city, where they had numerous kinsmen. His description of family life (*vida em família*) among these upper-class kinsmen and their in-laws, both in the community of Vila Recôncavo and in the city, is reminiscent of descriptions of family life in the nineteenth century.

The parentela of the other social classes differs strikingly, however, from that of the upper class. Although members of Class B take "as their pattern the older traditions of the upper-class families" (Hutchinson, H.W. 1957:137), they do not, with only one exception, have numerous kinsmen (1957:135), but "are conjugal units without local tradition of generations in the area" (1957:135), for they are apt to be people from other communities or newly arrived socially. Little is said about the extended kinship relations of Class C, but it must be presumed that, like the slaves before them, wage workers on the plantations and the lower class in the town seldom have more than a few relatives. Yet as in the past, the permanent fieldhands on the family-run plantations are, in a sense, attached to the families of the plantation owner, for a strong sense of paternalism persists in Vila Recôncavo. Class D is characterized by fragile marital bonds, often by women without husbands, and the kinship ties are few.

As might be expected, the members of the landowning class in Vila Recôncavo use the compadrio system to reinforce their already widespread kinship bonds (Hutchinson, H.W. 1957: 130). On the contrary, Class C, lacking the support of kinsmen, looks for compadres in the upper class. "If possible, at least one of the godparents will be a member of the upper class, a patron who will help the child if necessary, especially if the godson when he grows up wants to go to school in the city or enter the army or navy" (Hutchinson, H.W. 1957:147).

CERRADO AND RETIRO (Costa 1955:132–46)

Cerrado, a small town of 2,425 inhabitants, is the county seat of a large *município* (county) of nearly 13,000 people. Retiro, where approximately 400 people live, consists of a group of ranches within this same município. Cerrado and Retiro are both situated in the upper São Francisco Valley in the state of Minas Gerais. The economic life of this community depends primarily on the grazing of cattle, but there is also considerable subsistence agriculture (maize, beans, and rice), some production of cotton for export, and some mining of rock crystal.

Borges Costa makes a clear distinction between the household unit, consisting of the nuclear family in the majority of cases, and the parentela. The term *família* may be used for either unit, but often it is used to mean a subunit of the parentela (that is, the nuclear family of the ego, of his uncles and aunts, of his grandparents, of his cousins, and of his nephews and nieces). The parentela, he states, "is more cohesive than any other association such as political parties, economic associations, or cliques" (Costa 1955:141). Such large groups are known by certain surnames (such as the Oliveiras and the Barbosas), but in the traditional manner, people are given surnames in a variety of ways, mainly to indicate their kinship with a strong parentela (Costa 1955:146). Social life is intimate within such groups. Kinsmen back up kinsmen in crisis situations such as death, financial loss, and the like; and for birthdays and weddings "relatives . . . are always present to cooperate in the preparations" (Costa 1955:142).

The cohesion of political parties depends on the parentelas that make them up. "The Ferreira family always was of Party A," writes Borges Costa (1955:144). "Recently, when one of its members had almost decided to vote for a candidate of Party B, he was reprehended severely by his godfather, who is the political leader [of Party A], and also by his uncle."

Fueds still continue in Cerrado between families; two family groups have been for some years in open conflict, which is only periodically interrupted. Recently there was a shooting in the streets between members of these families (Costa 1955:143). Members of these families feel the responsibility of avenging offenses and even slights shown toward family members. Judicial and police authorities (often "outsiders") have been forced to leave the community in fear of their lives because they offended a member of a large parentela. (Costa 1955: 143). In Cerrado and Retiro, "it is dangerous to speak badly

about anybody when others are standing nearby, because
these might be kinsmen, however remote, of the person in
question" (Costa 1955:142).

The size of these parentelas is not given, although they
would seem to be very large. Differences in kinship extension
according to social classes are not mentioned, yet it is clear
from the study that they are present in both the urban (Cerrado) and the rural (Retiro) area.

PASSAGEM GRANDE (Araujo 1955:113–31)

In this small community (population 3,713) in the northeastern state of Alagoas, the cultivation of rice is the principal
basis of the economy. The majority of the population are wage
workers on the rice farms, and this is a zone of heavy migration to the cities and to the rural areas of the "south" (mainly
São Paulo). A large parentela, or "extended family" as Maynard Araujo calls it, is characteristic of only one "dominant
family." The number of relatives of this kinship circle "adds up
to more than a hundred members." Despite marriages between
relatives (cousins with cousins), it is the family with the
largest number of members (Araujo 1955:113). There is, however, a division among them into "poor" and "rich" relatives—
the "poor relatives" are the "children of a brother of the family
head who died—leaving his young children" in the hands of
the widow, who does not know how to take care of their
economic interests. The present "family head" owns several
rice farms, which are administered by his three sons-in-law.
"His sons . . . were not interested in the life of a 'hick' [ma-
tuto] and went to study in the capital, . . ." and after graduation evidently stayed there. Even among the upper classes who
own considerable rural property, the size of the parentela is
reduced by migration to large cities.

In Passagem Grande the parentela of the lower . socioeconomic groups suffers most intensely from migration and is

thus relatively circumscribed. One man, a barber, was able to enumerate forty-five relatives in the community. Another lower-class man listed twenty-eight relatives including his "wife and eleven children" but added that "in the south, if they are alive, I have five brothers" and an unknown number of sisters-in-law and nephew and nieces. Still another informant had sixty-three local relatives but again spoke of his two brothers in the "south" of whom he "never had news." The desirability of a large parentela was made explicit by one informant who complained about his lack of kinsmen: "I am envious of Sebastião," he said, "that one has a *parentada* [kinship group] which is a 'beauty' [*beleza*]—I think almost a hundred."

MINAS VELHAS (Harris 1956)

Minas Velhas is a small county seat in the mountain area of central Bahia State. It was once the commercial center of a region prosperous for gold and diamond mining. Today it is a bureaucratic and commercial town; subsistence farmers make up the surrounding population.

The parentela functions with much-diminished force in Minas Velhas, despite the fact that it is a relatively isolated community proud of its old traditions. The sharp decline of its old mining economy and the rise in social position of the local artisans have modified the old social structure. Yet the community still holds the remnants of a regional aristocracy consisting of three *famílias* represented by approximately 11 per cent of the population. This local upper class (which would be middle class in the city) has been "connected and reconnected" within itself and with other famílias in other communities of the region. It is still obviously the dominant group in local economics (Harris 1956:107–8), and it has traditionally dominated local politics, although one family called the Bomfims has split politically to the point "that first cousins meeting on the street fail to acknowledge each other" (Harris 1956:151). Although the size of these parentelas of the local elite is not specified, they are large, extending into other communities and even to the city of Salvador, to which many of them have migrated.

Even among the average townsmen in Minas Velhas, the network of kin is relatively large. "Almost any townsman can name up to one hundred kin living in Minas Velhas or in the vicinity," among whom are many relatives of the second and third degree (Harris 1956:148–49). And close kin particularly "treat each other with special deference, visit each other, borrow and lend feely and count upon each other for mutual support in crisis situations" (Harris 1956:149). Yet in Minas Velhas such parentelas are often divided by political, economic, and social lines. Beyond the primary relatives (parents, siblings, grandparents, aunts and uncles, and first cousins), kinship ties are but weakly considered. However, in Minas Velhas those same people who lack strong kinship ties make full use of the compadrio system in an effort to extend the realm of quasi-kin. Only among the upper class are compadres selected to reinforce kinship ties; among groups of the middle and lower classes people select their children's godparents from among the influential elite who might tender assistance to the child and to themselves. Thus, ten men, the heads of upper-class households, had a total of 336 godchildren (plus twice as many compadres) among them. Although as Harris points out, obligations assumed in compadrio systems are not taken in their full traditional meanings and are often "flimsy and artificial," kinship bonds are extended by the compadrio system.

ITÁ (Wagley 1953)

In 1948, the community of Itá consisted of a small town (a county seat) of approximately 600 people, and the surrounding

rural population of about 2,000. It is situated on the lower
Amazon River in the State of Pará. The town is an administrative and commercial center; the rural population is divided
between subsistence farmers—who are mainly cultivators of
manioc—and collectors of wild rubber. Before 1912 the town
was a prosperous commercial center for the rubber trade; but
with the end of the Amazon rubber boom, it declined in importance and in population. Most of the traditional families,
including that of the Baron of Itá, have left to seek a living
elsewhere.

In 1948 Itá had a small "first class" (local upper class),
which comprised remnants of the traditional families, merchants, public employees, and officials. It had a lower class
consisting of three segments—rural farmers, rubber gatherers,
and the lower-class town dwellers who did manual labor of
one kind or another. The "first class" explicitly expressed the
ideal of large parentelas and told of the old days, when local
society boasted great families that controlled economic, social,
and political life. But their kinsmen were few, because most of
them had moved away (Wagley 1953b:148). Likewise, the
lower-class townsmen had few kinsmen in the community, for
many of their brothers and cousins had left for the city or
other parts of the state to look for employment. Members of
the rural population devoted to rubber collecting were known
for their nomadic habits. They moved whenever possible to
escape debts and with the hope of finding a more productive
rubber trail to exploit (Wagley 1953b:149). Thus their local
kinsmen were few. And since both of these lower-class groups
were largely illiterate, they tended to lose contact with their
kinsmen in other communities.

This situation, however, did not hold true for a settlement of
small farmers. In the settlement of Jocojó, within the Itá community, a complex web of kinship ties united the inhabitants of

the nineteen households. One man, the leader, claimed kinship with 80 of the 102 people; and another counted 50 as consanguineous relatives and many more as affinals. In Itá only the relatively stable farming population, less affected by the ups and downs of the rubber market, had a large network of kin.

In the absence of large parentelas, the compadrio system functions to almost exaggerated proportions. People have the usual compadres of baptism, confirmation, and marriage. In addition there are "Compadres of the Fire." Members of the first class had an average of 28.1 godchildren, while members of the lower class averaged only 4.2 godchildren. In addition, all of them had many "Compadres of the Fire," a less serious relationship. As might be expected, nonkin were selected as compadres in Itá in almost all cases.

CRUZ DAS ALMAS (Pierson 1948)

Cruz das Almas (population 2,723, of which 90 per cent live in the village), only twenty-four miles from the great city of São Paulo, is a village of relatively stable and homogeneous small farmers. In the past a few plantation-owning families provided the community with an upper class, but they have either migrated or been reduced in status (Pierson 1952:202). Thus today there is no local or regional upper class. In this essentially one-class community, the kinship ties are strong.

"In this community," writes Donald Pierson (1952:127), "individuals are bound together in families with tenacious bonds of belonging, obligation, and affection, which by way of inter-family marriage extend throughout virtually the entire community." The size of such groups is large. One twenty-four-year-old woman, cited as an example, recalled without effort 166 relatives. Among these relatives, sixty-four had the same surname as the informant, but sixteen other surnames—including the six most common surnames of the village—were found in her list. Futhermore, people extend their kinship ties through the compadrio system. Of twenty-five persons questioned as to how many godchildren they had, none had less than one and one person had forty. One villager who prepared a list of compadres for Pierson listed fifty-three, of whom seven were relatives and forty-six were nonkinsmen.

In discussing the functions of the family, Pierson stresses the more immediate groups of the nuclear and patriarchal family of a man, his sons, and their spouses; yet it is quite evident that the large parentela is of considerable importance in community affairs. One village leader made this quite clear in his statement referring to a coming election. "I have the key that controls the community," he said. "I have fifty-three compadres. Besides, there are my relatives, my children, my sons-in-law, my daughters-in-law, my nephews and nieces. Here in these parts, the Buenos and the Cardosos [the names of his own and his wife's families] é mato [are legion]. That's why no one here can win from me. Every election it is the same; if I go one way, you can bet they'll go with me and that we'll win" (Pierson 1952:184–85). Membership in a prominent family that has been in the community a long time is listed as one of the more important criteria that make for high prestige (Pierson 1952:202).

CUNHA (Willems 1947)

Situated in the coastal range of São Paulo State, Cunha is the name of a county (município) and the county seat. The county contains over 25,000 people, of which only some 6,500 live in the city. It is a region of subsistence farming, producing mainly maize and beans. In recent years the exhausted soils have been turned more and more to pasture. The natural increase in population, combined with the inefficient agricultural system and the growth of grazing, has caused an exodus from Cunha to other communities and to the city of São Paulo. In nine "traditional" families selected at random, 25.9 per cent of the members lived outside the community. According to Emilio Willems, local society contains three socio-economic classes—an upper class made up of the "traditional families" as well as of some outsiders (even foreigners) and their descendants who have achieved a secure economic and social position; a middle class whose members are lower in the social and economic scale but who, because of their education, occupations, and manners, maintain cordial relations with the upper class; and finally the lower class made up of sharecroppers, renters, poor farmers, artisans, and manual laborers.

Both the older rural *bairros* (districts) and the city "were inhabited by families, largely related." Of the 296 individuals measured by Willems for his studies in physical anthropology (1947:56–57), 127 carried only 17 traditional surnames, and there were 33 people known by 1 surname and 27 by another. And among the 9 families from which he drew his data on migration, it is clear that each listed an average of 135 relatives, over 100 of them in the community. One family listed a total of 435 relatives from 6 generations, another 274 from 4 generations, and 1 only 10 relatives from 2 generations (Willems 1947:52). Willems notes the "respect" offered to relatives, even though removed, and the solidarity among relatives that surpasses that of mere neighbors (1947:56). Kinship seems to have provided a bridge between the town and the rural zones. "Almost all the great families residing in the *sêde* [county seat] have ramifications in the rural zone, forming not infrequently enormous kinship circles [parentelas] in various districts" (Willems 1947:77).

It seems clear that kinship was still important in Cunha society. Yet, evidently, family oligarchies had, at the time the study was carried out, lost control in local politics. The deterioration of a traditional system of common landholding among siblings had made for conflicts between relatives. The loss of what was locally called *respeito* (literally "respect," but actually "a sense of solidarity") had produced disorganization in the family or parentela (Willems 1947:55). And this was supplemented by the exodus of kinsmen from the community.

CONCLUSIONS:

It is evident from the data provided by these seven community studies that kinship plays an important role in social, economic, and even political affairs. Yet it is equally apparent that not all of the various social and economic classes that make up these communities share the large parentela. In the communities under review three social segments seem to be characterized by widely extended kinship networks—the descendants of the landed gentry (Vila Recôncavo), the local elite (Minas Velhas, Cerrado and Retiro, Passagem Grande, and Cunha), and the stable subsistence farmers (Itá and Cruz das Almas). It is the wage workers on plantations, sharecroppers, rubber gatherers, and others whose economic condition is unstable and precarious who seem singularly to lack kinsmen. Yet, even these lower-class groups are often connected with important parentelas in the communities in which they live Although the obligations involved have been attenuated, the compadrio system is used more widely to secure protection by those without kinsmen. In none of these communities, with the possible exception of Vila Recôncavo, does the parentela assume the form of the patriarchal family of the past, yet kinship ties retain many of their former essential functions.

Objective and empirical data as to the extension of kinship ties and the role of kinship are less readily available for those segments of the Brazilian population not included in the communities studied above. It would seem probable that kinship would be less extensive in recently settled frontier regions. The same would seem to be true also in great cities among lower-class groups, so many of which have migrated recently from small towns and rural zones. Yet it is always possible that migration from one region to another and from rural districts to urban zones may involve not isolated individuals or nuclear families but whole parentelas.

For one urban class, the urban upper class, however, there are clear indications that kinship has very important ramifications. In Salvador, Carmelita Junqueira Ayres Hutchinson (1955:268) reports one member of an important and traditional family who was able to name and give the precise genealogical relationship of 290 kinsmen (53 of whom were deceased). According to Mrs. Hutchinson, this is not unusual among the Baian upper classes. A series of interviews carried out among the middle and upper classes in Rio de Janeiro shows that individuals maintain relations with between 100 and 200 relatives, and people related to wealthy and traditional parentelas often recognize even more numerous kinsmen (Wagley, Field Notes). And, in the city of São Paulo, Emilio Willems (1953:343) states that people "were able to distinguish between 30 and 500 relatives." In these large cities crowded urban conditions have dispersed kinsmen throughout the city, but such conditions have not isolated them from one another. Regular telephone conversations, frequent visiting, and many "family" gatherings at weddings, baptisms, graduation ceremonies, birthdays, and the like maintain these large parentelas in an intimate and continuous relationship. And there is a trend, often commented on but as yet unstudied to my knowledge, for kinsmen to purchase or rent apartments in one building, uniting a segment of the parentela under the same roof. Large, elite kin groups still dominate Brazilian economics and are important in politics. An American economist writing about Brazil a few years ago said, "The power of the oligopolis and the duopolis is enhanced by the strong ties which exist among the few families that are strong in business and politics" (Spiegel 1949:228).

The other social classes of the great urban centers of Brazil do not share, in practice, the large parentela. Members of the middle class are often migrants from provincial cities and small towns. They often help their kinsmen to migrate to the city and they maintain contact with their kinsmen at home. The lower class in the big cities suffers most from the lack of kinsmen. They come from far away and they are often illiterate; thus they lose contact with their relatives on plantations and small farms. It is this segment of Brazilian society, more than any other, that seems to lack the support of a wide network of kinsmen. But even for these people, the large parentela persists as an image or an ideal—as the way people ought to behave and ought to live in Brazil. Whenever possible they attach themselves to families and they extend their kin by the compadrio system. As one very astute Brazilian writer put it, "The patriarchal system still impregnates the minds of Brazilians, even when they are no longer able to live it out" (Tavaris de Sá 1947:10).

This tradition of familism has deep roots in the Portuguese tradition. Jorge Dias (1955:13) comments on this historical fact and describes the extended family (or the parentela) in modern Portugal in the following terms:

The relations beween the members of families (i.e., *parentelas*) are always highly intimate and sometimes exclusive. Parents and children, brothers and sisters, uncles and aunts, cousins of both sexes form closed and confused networks into which an outsider penetrates with difficulty. Many of these *familias* meet together frequently. On birthdays—of the oldest as well as of the youngest —the whole *familia* comes together, often bringing with them servants to take care of the children. Christmas, New Years, Easter, and the other principal festivals of the year are always pretexts for "get-togethers" when the family is invited for lunch, for dinner, or for tea after which conversation goes on around the table or in other rooms when it is an upper-class family.

Jorge Dias' description would be valid for the provincial upper class of small towns and cities of Brazil today as well as for many Brazilians who live in great metropolitan centers.

The persistence of the widely extended parentela in Brazil must be considered as the reflection of deep-seated Luso-Brazilian values. The patriarchal family system of the plantation era may have disappeared, yet the strong bonds of kinship have been re-formed in terms of contemporary conditions of life. The traditional emphasis on the family and the parentela provides a model for human relations that is an aspiration for even those segments of the society that cannot live in this way. The predominance of kinship in ordering social life explains the relative absence in Brazil of such voluntary associations as parent-teacher groups, garden clubs, civic clubs, and the like. People give greater value to kinship relations than to relations based on common interest or even occupation.

Recently Arnold Strickon has shown that the working-class rural criollo of Argentina depends strongly on a large kinship group extending his relations horizontally by affinity—recognizing all of his *cuñados* and *concuñados* as well as all his *parientes* within the realm of his knowledge. He says, "Jobs and assistance of various kinds depend upon some kinds of kin tie to the person who has them to dispose, making it advantageous to extend one's kinship network as widely as possible" (Strickon 1962:514). He also points out that the Argentine elite extend their kinsmen vertically—that is, in a lineal system, deriving from some famous or wealthy man on the mother's as well as the father's side. This also makes for a large kindred similar to that found in Brazil. There is no doubt in my mind that the kindred rather than the more immediate family is one of the fundamental institutions of Latin American society. In each nation it needs to be studied by economists interested in business enterprise, by political scientists interested in the actual function of government, by historians interested in regional or local developments, and by all of us interested in Latin American society. The persistence of kinship in Brazilian society, or in any Latin American society, should be viewed not as a social or cultural lag but rather as the continuation of a fundamental cultural value. There is a growing body of evidence that kinship relations and awareness of kinship need not disappear with industrialization and urbanization. Our own situation in the United States, where kinship is reduced to a minimum in channeling social relations, may be a result "of the presence of the small family in Northern Europe prior to the industrial revolution," and not a functional result of the industrialization or urbanization (Greenfield 1961:322). There is every reason to believe that, especially in those cultures where the tradition of familism has been strong, such as Brazil and other countries of Latin America, kinship will continue to play an important role in ordering social relations. A true comparative sociology cannot be based on the United States and northern Europe alone; it must consider the different cultural traditions of the "new" countries.

[VII]

THE DILEMMA OF THE LATIN AMERICAN MIDDLE CLASS

THE nineteenth-century concept of Latin American class structure no longer is valid. Latin American nations are not composed nowadays of a landed gentry versus a mass of illiterate peons, mestizos, Indians, colonos, sharecroppers, or squatters. Most Latin American nations are today infinitely more complex in social structure. Whether it is the result of industrialization, the growth of great cities, mechanization of agriculture, or other processes of modernization, new social groups have appeared, and there has been a fundamental realignment of social classes.

In the last generation or so, a new sector of industrialists and businessmen have appeared in such countries as Mexico, Venezuela, Colombia, Peru, Chile, Argentina, Uruguay, and Brazil. In most countries they are today more important in the national power structure than the traditional landholding and rural-based elite. Likewise, with the growth of industry a significant urban working class has appeared. And, also, most

This paper was given first as an address at the spring meeting of the Academy of Political Science (May 5, 1964) at Columbia University. It appeared in print, in a different form, in the *Proceedings of the Academy of Political Science* (Vol. XXVII, May 1964, No. 4, pp. 2–10), New York.

Latin American cities contain a large mass of mainly rural migrants who inhabit the *barriadas, favelas, invasões,* or *callampas*—the enormous shantytowns. In the rural areas there is an enlarged rural proletariat—the wage workers on the large mechanized plantations—producing sugar, coffee, bananas, cacao, cotton, and other commercial crops. Finally there is a new Latin American middle class that has come to have an increasing voice in the life of many nations. It is the purpose of this paper to identify this new middle class and to point out some of its real problems. It is my thesis that this sector of the Latin American population is caught up in a dilemma between its liberal democratic ideals and the realities involved in the extension of liberal democracy—between a desire to extend the benefits of modern technology to the whole body politic and the terrible cost of doing so.

The presence of a middle class patterned on the model of those which exist in western Europe and the United States has been doubted or denied by many analysts of Latin American society. Most observers agree on the rapid increase both numberically and strategically of a "middle group," a "middle mass," a "middle sector," a "middle strata," or another term that dodges the word "class." It is pointed out, however, that this sector in Latin American societies is heterogeneous in origin. Some of the members of this "class" derive from the old elite who have declined economically from the position once held by their ancestors. Others are of middle class origin; still others are immigrants or children of immigrants. A few have lower class origins. Economically they range from wealthy businessmen to small shopkeepers and, in terms of education, from highly trained technicians and professors with Ph.D. degrees to people who have not completed primary school. It is also pointed out that these middle groups lack a class consciousness and a class ideology. These people are apt to model themselves in social behavior and cultural values after the old aristocracy. They place great value on a white-collar occupation, even though it may pay less than skilled manual labor; they value classical literary education over technical and scientific training; they tend toward conspicuous consumption and even ostentation. These middle groups from this point might best be viewed as marginal to an enlarged upper class.

This view of the Latin American middle groups was certainly true in the nineteenth and early twentieth centuries and it may still be true in many Latin American countries. Yet it seems to me that we should recognize that in certain Latin American countries such as Argentina, Chile, Uruguay, Brazil, Mexico, and Venezuela, a middle class of sizeable proportions now exists with a distinctive way of life and its own self-identity as well as an objective middle position in the economic structure of the nation. Its emergence as a rather large and distinctive group is recent and is part of the massive social and political change in process in most of Latin America.

WHO IS MIDDLE CLASS IN LATIN AMERICA?

Who are these people who I believe belong to a middle class rather than to an amorphous "middle mass" or "middle sector"? Several writers dubious of the existence of a Latin American middle class speak of an upper and lower middle sector or class. The upper middle class consists of people of some wealth —businessmen, managers, high level and successful professionals, and high level bureaucrats and politicians. They are not quite wealthy enough to belong to the new upper class; they lack the family background of the traditional elite. In fact, they may be immigrants or the children of immigrants. But this is the group, in my opinion, which shares the aristocratic values of the upper class. These people can afford to join the same clubs and to send their children to the same schools as those attended by the children of the upper class. They are upwardly mobile and ambitious. The successful sons of this "upper middle sector" often marry into elite families. They are, in a sense, a recognizable group—a marginal sector of the upper class.

It is those people who can be classed in the lower "middle sectors" or strata who are a new phenomenon in Latin American society and who have the characteristics of a middle class that sets them off from the elite. It is this group that I shall speak of as the middle class in the pages that follow.

Members of the middle class share a series of common qualities. First, they have white-collar occupations, but not the most lucrative or prestigeful ones. They are small businessmen, professionals of various sorts (dentists, pharmacists, not-so-successful lawyers, physicians, engineers, and the like). Above all they are salaried workers—employees of banks and business firms, teachers in primary and secondary schools, and government employees. Artisans and other skilled workers, even though they earn more money than many of the middle class, are considered lower class. In fact the middle class is poorly paid—although when the average income is compared to the average income of the lower classes, they are wealthy. In 1962 a middle class Chilean might make as much as two hundred dollars per month (Guzzardi 1962). In Brazil at about the same time such individuals would have been fortunate to earn four hundred cruzeiros (about twenty dollars) per month, but this was several times the salary paid to laborers.

Second, the middle class is overwhelmingly urban because this class is, in a sense, the result of industrial and commercial development. Few small farmers, except perhaps in southern Brazil, Antioquia (Colombia), and Costa Rica, could be counted members of the middle class. But in all small towns there is a local elite—government employees, storekeepers, clergy, and others who are "white collar"—who, from a national perspective, can be considered members of the middle class. Even the middle class living in small towns has an urban ethos—it is turned away from the rural zone toward the city in its thinking (Harris 1956:279 ff.).

Third, members of the Latin American middle class are literate. Their education may range from a few years of primary school to a university degree. This means several things. They value education for their children and believe strongly in universal public education. They are also consumers of newspapers and magazines including such foreign imports as *Life en Espanol* and *Seleciones* (*Readers Digest*). Because the electoral laws of most Latin American nations require literacy, only the middle and upper classes vote. The middle class is well aware of political events and problems, although it may not altogether understand them.

Fourth, the Latin American middle class is traditionalistic and nationalistic. While the lower class shares almost vicariously in national traditions, this middle class is anxious to live them out. While the upper class (and the upper-middle class) have cosmopolitan tastes and manners (that is, French and North American), members of the middle class attempt to retain Latin American tastes and manners of behavior—they express "Mexicanidad," the Gaucho spirit of Argentina and Uruguay; the Bandeirante spirit of São Paulo (Brazil); and other forms of creolisms throughout the continent. In terms of ideal patterns of behavior they value large kinship groups (parentela), respect for the obligations and rights of their compadres, a dual role for the sexes (*machismo* for males and virginity before marriage for girls), and other traditional Latin American ideal patterns today often honored in the breach. (See Chapter II.)

THE MIDDLE CLASS AND NATIONALISM

The middle class is not only nationalistic but its members have a most vociferous voice. The elite (and upper-middle class) are likely to be cosmopolitan; the lower class is likely to be relatively unaware of nationalistic symbols. The middle class is fully cognizant of all the stereotypes and symbols of nationalism. Their nationalism tends to have a negative aspect. A great Mexican historian has described Latin American nationalism: "It was seldom born or suckled by faith in its own values, but was born, grew, and flourished as a reaction of protest, suspicion, and even hatred and contempt for the wrongs done by foreign individuals, companies, and governments" (Cosio Villegas 1963:122). This nationalism, he adds, "in the last twenty years—reached incredible extremes of emotion and irrationality."

In the past, Great Britain, France, and Germany, as well as the United States were the butts of this suspicion and hatred, but today the United States is the principal scapegoat. Hundreds of thousands of the Latin American middle class may study English in binational centers sponsored by the United States government; they may also be eager to study in colleges and universities in the United States; they may be addicts of North American music, movies, and novels (in translation); but they are anti-American. They believe that United States corporations plot to exploit their countries' raw materials. They point out penetration of American firms into commerce and industry. They distrust, with some reason, the foreign policy of the United States government. They fear intervention, and they point out that U.S. foreign aid comes with strings attached.*

---

* One of the most widely circulated and cited books in Latin America in the last few years was John Gerassi's *The Great Fear* (1963) which is a rather shrill exposé of U.S.A. intrigue in Latin America.

Yet there is also a positive side of this Latin American nationalism which is again expressed most articulately by the middle class. A generation or so ago, the Latin American upper class and the small peripheral middle class looked to Europe, sometimes to the United States, for almost all they admired. They were ashamed of the non-European aspects of their own national cultures. For example, Mexico rejected the Indian and the mestizo. Today these sectors of the Mexican population stand as symbols of the Mexican Revolution. Twenty years ago a Guatemalan lady of the upper or middle class would not have been "caught dead in" a dress made of local fabric with an Indian design; today, "Indian inspired" fabrics made in Guatemala are a source of national pride. Brazil has gone through a veritable about-face in this regard in the last twenty years. Before, the middle class was ashamed of life in the backlands and of its African heritage. Nowadays, books, music, and movies such as *Black Orpheus* (a story of the favellas) and *The Man Who Fulfilled His Vows* (a story of religious fanaticism in the backlands and of the African candomble ceremonies of Bahia) are exported with pride. This positive aspect of nationalism has given the middle class a pride in itself, a self-respect, and the courage to value its own national traditions.

HOW LARGE IS THE MIDDLE CLASS?

It seems self-evident to me that the middle class is a distinctive and recently emerged sector of Latin American society. It seems evident, too, that they are numerically important in certain countries and in certain regions of some countries. But these are impressions gained by reading, visiting, and casual observation. It is very difficult to estimate their numerical strength partly because of the criteria of the middle class which I have discussed above. There have been several educated guesses as to the numerical strength of the middle class in various Latin American countries, but most often such estimates have defined the middle class in terms of both an upper and lower strata. Most writers include the wealthy industrialist and the high level administrator with the shopkeeper and the government or business office clerk. Using this broader definition (he calls it "middle sector"), J. J. Johnson (1958:2) estimates that 35 per cent of the people of Argentina, 30 per cent of Chile and Uruguay, 15–20 per cent of Brazil; and 12 per cent of Venezuela are classified as members of the middle class.

Gino Germani and Kalman Silvert using a broad definition of middle class also provide us with a classification of Latin American countries in regard to the strength of the middle class. (Germani 1962:169; Germani and Silvert 1965:247–48.) They classify the various nations in four groups. Group A is made up of Argentina, Uruguay, Chile, and Costa Rica. This group has a middle strata of 20 per cent or more. This is a middle class with cultural, psychological, and political identity. Group B is made up of Mexico and Brazil with an approximate middle strata of between 15 and 20 per cent of the population. Although a middle class exists, it is highly concentrated in certain regions of each country (that is, in Mexico and other provincial capitals, and in south Brazil). Group C includes Cuba (pre-Castro), Venezuela, and Colombia. The estimated middle strata of these countries is also between 15 and 20 per cent, but they are considered to have only an emergent middle class. There is considerable disagreement as to the strength of self-identity among the middle strata in this group. And finally, there are all of the other countries with less than 15 per cent in the middle strata, with only a nascent "middle class" in some countries and a clear persistence of the traditional two-class system in others. In most of the countries with a small middle strata, a large proportion of the total population is marginal to the national economic and political life.

While neither Johnson's rough estimate of the "middle sectors" nor Germani and Silvert's more careful estimate of the "middle strata" gives any precise figures for the numerical strength of the "middle class," they do indicate the countries where the middle class is strongest—Argentina, Uruguay, Chile, Costa Rica, Mexico, Brazil, Venezuela, and Colombia. And perhaps Peru and Panama should be added to this list. In general, these are the countries with the highest indices of urbanization and the highest rate of literacy (Brazil is an exception). They are also the countries with the highest annual income per capita, although in 1961 this ranged in the countries mentioned above from $799.00 for Argentina to $361.60 for Costa Rica. It is also these same countries that are leaders in mass media—in newspaper circulation, cinemas, television and radio stations, and the publication of books and magazines (Rycroft and Clemen 1963).[*] It is quite clear that the size of the middle class corresponds closely with the degree of urbanization, industrialization, ethnic and cultural homogeneity, literacy, and the demand for public services. In other words, the larger the middle class in a Latin American nation, the greater the degree of technological, economic, and social modernization. However, it is to be noted at once that its presence in significant size in a nation does not correlate necessarily with political stability. Argentina, Brazil, and Venezuela —countries with relatively large middle classes—have been plagued with political difficulties during the last ten years or more. Colombia has suffered from terrible internal violence at least partially of political origin, and Cuba has experienced a communist revolution.

[*] The authors have made extensive use of United Nations Documents as well as other sources.

THE MIDDLE CLASS DILEMMA

This Latin American middle class finds itself in an economic, political, and social dilemma. The realities of present day Latin American society run contrary to the needs, the aspirations, and the ideology of this new social group. Although it holds many traditional values, the new middle class has modern needs and aspirations. But it is still living in a society in transition from a rural agrarian semifeudal and personalistic social system to an urban, industrial, impersonal social system.

Middle class people in Latin America are consumers. They are accustomed to adequate housing. Since they work in offices, classrooms, stores, and other public places in a white-collar capacity, they need to dress well. They want television sets, electric refrigerators, washing machines, and other accoutrements of the modern world. They would like to have an automobile if that were possible. But the realities of their economic situation are otherwise. Manufactured goods are expensive in any terms—because even if not imported, they are produced by a protected national industry. Rents, clothes, medicines, and even food are expensive for the poorly paid middle class. Between 1953 an 1960 the indices of cost of living rose from 100 to 436 in Rio de Janeiro, from 100 to 593 in Buenos Aires, from 100 to 1182 in Santiago, Chile (Centro Latino Americano de Pesquizas em Ciências Sociais 1961:124). Furthermore, inflation is constant, sometimes rampant, in countries with a significant middle class. The middle class lives on fixed income, almost always salaries, which lag behind the rising cost of living and are adjusted slowly in face of inflation. Middle class people are often heavily in debt.

There is only one answer to the economic dilemma of the Latin American middle class, namely, to make more money. Thus Latin American middle class men—teachers, poorly paid professionals, government employees, and others—"moonlight," holding down several jobs. It is common for a government employee to work also in a private firm. Obviously he neglects his relatively secure government job. It is common for professors in universities to teach in more than one faculty and for secondary school teachers to teach their subject in several schools. Furthermore, the budget of most middle class families in Latin America can only be balanced if there are several wage-earners contributing; thus, sons and daughters work while still studying, and it is more and more common for the wife to work.

The middle classes are also frustrated by the lack of public services in the cities in which they typically live. Public services have not been able to keep pace with the extremely rapid growth of cities; in some cases, they have actually deteriorated. The middle class spends endless hours waiting for infrequent and poor public transportation. They bear the lack of water and lack of telephones with amazing patience but also with irritation. Public services, until recently, were foreign owned. Nationalists were certain that foreign transportation and utility companies were extracting tremendous loot from their countries and in many cases this was probably so. Such corporations were not allowed to increase their rates and in turn they refused to improve facilities, expecting that they would be expropriated. By now most of them have been nationalized. But compensation to these foreign companies has put a heavy weight on countries which are short in foreign exchange. And, once nationalized, the public transportation and utilities were in poor condition. Water supply systems, sewers, roads, telephone systems, public transportation, and the other public services—which the middle class needs more than any other sector of the Latin American population—call for heavy capital expenditures. If this is to be done, then taxes must be increased. Neither the Latin American elite nor the middle class is accustomed to paying heavy direct taxes, but they are now learning. Increased taxes are an added burden to a middle class which hardly lives within its income. (I might add that this is not a distinctive Latin American phenomenon.)

As it is with public facilities, so it is with education. The Latin American middle class, as we have said, places a high value on education, and they want public schools for their children. They are no longer satisfied with just the primary education to which many of the present day adults were limited, and their children crowd into secondary schools and universities. Public primary schools are crowded; public secondary schools are too few in many cities. So the middle class must take on the extra cost of private secondary schools. They are willing to make sacrifices to allow their children to attend the university. Yet even though universities are almost free, most university students, especially those from the middle class, work as they study.

The dilemma of the Latin American middle class is not only material and economic. They are faced with ideological and cultural conflicts as well. They are traditionalists but they are also liberal democrats, and they believe that equality of opportunity should be extended to the mass of people in their countries. Their children may be university students who vibrate with nationalism and with the ideal of equal opportunity for all. Yet, given the relatively underdeveloped economy of their nations, to provide the same conditions of life for the mass of people which the middle class itself struggles to maintain might well destroy their relatively favored position. They may not be overtly aware of this dilemma but it lies ominously in the background.*

* José Nun, in a paper published in 1965 after the original version of this essay appeared, states this ideological dilemma precisely and vividly. "I refer," he writes, "to structural tension of the orientations of the middle sectors that want such conditions as: economic development *and* monetary stability; State protection *and* non-intervention; better public

A single example of what I mean will have to suffice. As stated several times, the Latin American middle class believes strongly in the extension of free public education to the entire population. In most Latin American countries, this is an ideal far from realized. It is estimated that in 1950, 49 per cent of the population of Latin America over fifteen years of age had never attended school or had dropped out before completing one year (Rycroft and Clemen 1963:146). The educational institutions of most countries were originally established for the elite—a very small proportion of the total population. The educational system inherited from the past provides a poor basis for the building of a system making education available to all. Then too, the well-known population explosion which in a generation or so more than doubled the number of Latin Americans (even greater in the school population), does not make the task easier. To make universal education a reality, a massive undertaking—of training teachers, building schools, and reorganizing the curricula—would be necessary. This would call for a financial outlay by the governments far beyond that now made for education. In the process, the quality of the existing schools would certainly deteriorate. If a rich nation such as the United States has such problems in racial integration of its schools, one can only imagine the problems most Latin American nations would face in assimilating the entire mass of people into its educational institutions. Although this is the stated ideal of the Latin American middle class, it has to settle for less.

---

services *and* tax reduction; increase of rural productivity *and* respect for rural property; freedom of opinion *and* repression of the manifestations of anti-status quo opinions; abolition of privileges *and* access to aristocratic drawing rooms; etc. All this must be encompassed in a phraseology able to attract the feared masses without alienating the protected oligarchy." "A Latin American Phenomenon: The Middle Class Military Coup" in *Trends in Social Science Research: A Conference Report,* Institute of International Studies, University of California, Berkeley, 1965, p. 82.

Furthermore, the Latin American middle class equivocates in its liberal democratic views. It favors universal suffrage and freely elected governments. Literacy is a qualification for voting in most of Latin America, thereby automatically disfranchising a large sector of most national populations. Although several writers have spoken of some sort of middle class alliance with the workers, the facts do not seem to support this theory. It may be true that for a time the Argentine middle class sided with Peron and the *"discamisados"* against the oligarchy, or that the Brazilian middle class supported Vargas and his Brazilian Labor Party (P.T.B.). But, at the time, the middle class felt that it was in control. They did not cogitate turning over the dominant political power to the workers. And the so-called "alliance" ended when the working groups took, or seemed to take, control.

The middle class has a real political dilemma. Middle class people are energetically interested in politics. They know and appreciate the power of government. In fact, a large percentage of them owe their very class position to the expansion of government bureaucracy. They believe in honesty and morality in politics and in government. They are perforce adherents of statism, for they are not convinced that capitalism and free enterprise will lead to social and economic development of their countries as it seems to have in the United States. But, with few exceptions (perhaps the Christian Democrats of Chile, Peru, and Venezuela, as examples), there are no political parties that clearly represent their interests despite the high sounding names of many Latin American parties (Social Democrat, Liberal Party, National Democratic Union, and so forth). With their dependence on the state, the Latin American middle class becomes jittery in face of rapid change and the increased power of the urban and rural masses. Faced with a crisis, the middle class acquiesces; it remains passive before a military coup that guarantees stability or it actively supports a political party or a coalition of parties aimed at stability rather than abrupt change. There is no guarantee at all that the development of a strong middle class in Latin America will lead to the strengthening of democratic institutions.*

THE CASE OF THE BRAZILIAN MIDDLE CLASS

Perhaps I may illustrate the economic, social, and political dilemma of the middle class by the case of the Brazilian middle class—a group .about which I have had considerable knowledge. The Brazilian middle class is not numerically the strongest in Latin America in relation to the total population of the country. But, since World War II, it has gained remarkably in numerical strength and in self-identity, especially in south Brazil—in Rio de Janeiro, São Paulo, Belo Horizonte, Porto Alegre and other rapidly growing cities. The Brazilian middle class has suffered, perhaps more intensely than their counterparts in other countries, all the ills we have described: lack of public facilities, crowded schools, and low salaries that do not keep up with rampant inflation. Furthermore, Brazil has suffered a series of political crises since 1954 when the ex-dictator and then elected President, Getulio Vargas, committed

* Again José Nun, in the article referred to above, explains acquiescence of the middle class very clearly: "The 'premature' extension of suffrage to the masses confronts the different sectors of the middle classes with the problem of competing for power both with the upper and with the lower classes. . . . Through increasingly powerful trade unions, the labor movement (usually reformist) pressures *against privileges*. Through experienced channels of influence, the traditional elite pressures to *preserve privileges*. The threat of socialism or populism on one hand; the threat of an oligarchical rule on the other hand, and, at the center, these middle classes that cannot stay in the middle. When the precarious alliances reach the point of rupture, . . . there is then a high probability that members of the army will be called to help and/or will come to the rescue of those middle class sectors with whom it tends to become increasingly identified. The reason for this . . . is that the armed forces seem to be today one of the better, if not the best, structured institutions of the middle class" (*Trends in Social Science Research: A Conference Report,* p. 91).

suicide. In 1961 there was the dramatic resignation of President Jânio Quadros, a man who seemed to have a basis of political support and whose political symbol "the broom that swept the house clean" was pleasing to middle class morality. Then, the elected vice-president, Joáo Goulart, was allowed by the Army to assume the Presidency only after a constitutional amendment establishing a parliamentary form of government was passed. This was done to curb Goulart's power. A plebiscite in 1963 returned the country to a presidential form of government restoring most of the executive powers.

The year 1963 and the first months of 1964 were marked with continual crisis in Brazil. In 1963 a series of strikes upset transportation and industrial production. Inflation continued at an increased rate. The cost of living is said to have increased 80 per cent in 1963.

In the first three months of 1964, it almost seemed that Brazil was in a state of chaos. The cruzeiro dropped in value from 600 to the dollar in January to 1360 in March. A new round of strikes broke out among the dock workers, the bank employees, the transportation workers, and others. President Goulart seemed to be seeking his support from labor, the peasants, and the students. He announced a series of "basic reforms"—including a land reform bill authorizing the federal government to expropriate unused lands along highways, railroads, and waterways. He signed a bill lowering the rates on rent control. He was said to favor granting legality to the Brazilian Communist Party and there were discussions about the feasibility of recognition of Communist China. Goulart also announced that he was in favor of amending the Constitution of 1946 to grant suffrage to illiterates and to allow military personnel to run for elective office by placing themselves on inactive status. (Several noncommissioned officers had petitioned for this right.) There was a round of increases for labor but little help for the low-level white-collar worker. The middle class suffered and they were frightened.

There was a strong reaction from the middle class (and the upper class). *O Estado de São Paulo* and *O Globo*, conservative papers of wide circulation, warned of "socialist" and "communist" policies of Goulart's government. Carlos Lacerda, the Governor of Guanabara state in which Rio de Janeiro is situated and a critic of almost all federal regimes, fanned the flames by spectacular speeches over television lasting for hours. Anti-communist groups called for demonstrations in the streets to protest against the leftist trends of the Goulart government. In March of 1964 an estimated 500,000 people in São Paulo took part in a "God and Family" protest. Stories of the influence of China, Russia, and Cuba among the peasants in north Brazil were rife. It was rumored that Goulart planned to declare himself a dictator of the left. The middle class (and certain elements of the upper class) were in near panic.

The result is well known. Set off by a "sit down strike" or "mutiny" among 1425 enlisted men and noncommissioned officers which Goulart supported on March 31, 1964, the Brazilian Army took over the national government of Brazil within 24 hours. There was almost no resistance. Reportedly over 7000 people were arrested in a few days following the take-over, including important legislators and officials. On the evening of the coup, tons of paper was thrown from the windows of apartment houses and office buildings—obviously by people of the middle class. White candles of victory were lighted in middle-class apartment windows in Rio de Janeiro. And a march of protest similar to that which was carried out in São Paulo became a march of victory a day or so later. Evidently the middle class was pleased; it was relieved to have the military take over.

In the first months after the March 31 "revolution," the middle class seemed to give it its support despite the numerous actions contrary to middle class liberal democratic ideology. On April 9, 1966, the military command proclaimed the first Institutional Act (two more have followed) decreeing that "the victorious revolution dictates juridical powers without being limited in this right by the norms existing prior to its victory." On April 11, 1966, contrary to the existing Constitution, Marshal Humberto Castelo Branco was elected by the Chamber of Deputies as President of Brazil to serve until January 1966 (later extended one year). In the first two months, some four hundred people lost their political rights, among them three ex-Presidents and six state governors. These governors, fifty-five federal legislators, public officials, labor leaders, and others were included among those who lost the right to vote, to run for public office, or to hold government jobs. Despite the trappings of a Congress and Senate, a civilian ministry, and an "elected" president, this was clearly government by the military.

The new government seriously attempted to curb inflation with only moderate success. In 1965 it allowed three state elections; anti-government candidates won in the two important states of Minas Gerais and Guanabara. This indication of loss of support, particularly in states with an articulate middle class, led the government to tighten control. Political parties were abolished and a "Pro-Revolutionary" coalition was formed. (As yet there is no true opposition coalition.) It was decreed that the forthcoming election for Presidency and State Governments would be indirect by the legislation. This was followed by further *cassocões* (cancellations) of political rights seemingly to guarantee the election of government candidates. A "revolutionary" General, Costa e Silva, who was Minister of War, announced his candidacy for President and he was elected virtually without opposition. It looks as if the Brazilian government will be dominated by the military for many years to come. If this should happen, then the middle class will have made a bad bargain. As a result of its basic economic, social, and political dilemma, the Brazilian middle class opted for stability over change.

CONCLUSIONS

What happened in Brazil from 1964 to the present is not a unique phenomenon in Latin America. In its essential features, it has happened again and again—in Argentina, Colombia, Ecuador, Dominican Republic, Peru, and Venezuela. After initial support of a military regime which promised stability, the middle class found itself prisoner of a quasi-authoritarian state. And in Cuba what seemed to begin as a middle class revolution against the dictator became a communist revolution which has driven most of the middle class into exile. In all of these situations, the middle class might have been the crucial element for social and political change. It was not so; rather it faltered and acquiesced in favor of the status quo.

The Latin American middle class must solve its dilemma. It must decide to promote social and economic change and to build a society in its own image, no matter what the cost. And it will be a costly and difficult task to extend education, health, food, public services, and the right to vote to the mass of people. The middle class will itself suffer in the process. But the alternative is to live in a nation policed by the military or face a left-wing authoritarian regime which would aim at its destruction. The question facing the next generation in Latin America is whether or not the middle class is willing to pay the price of a peaceful revolution.

BIBLIOGRAPHICAL REFERENCES

Adams, Richard N.
1956 Cultural components of Central America. American Anthropologist 58:881–907.
1965 Introduction. Social Organization. *In* Contemporary Cultures of Latin America, edited by Dwight Heath and Richard Adams. New York, Random House.

Adams, Richard N. (Editor)
1957 Political changes in Guatemalan Indian Communities. Middle American Research Institute. Tulane University, pp. 1–54.

Aguirre Beltrán, Gonzalo
1940 La población Negra de México, 1519–1810. México, D. F. Ediciones Fuente Cultural.

Araujo, Alceu Maynard
1955 A família numa comunidade alagoana. Sociologia, XVIII (2).

Arensberg, Conrad
1961 The community as an object and as a sample. American Anthropologist, 63(2) part I:241–64.

Arias, B. Jorge
1961 Aspectos demográficos de la población indígena de Guatemala. Guatemala Indigena, I(2). Guatemala.

Barnes, John A.
1954 Class and committees in a Norwegian Island parish. Human Relations, VII(1): 39–58.

Beals, Ralph
1955   Indian-Mestizo-White relations in Spanish America. *In* Race Relations in World Perspective, edited by Andrew W. Lind. Honolulu, pp. 412–32.

Benjamin, Harold
1965   Higher education in the Americas. New York, McGraw-Hill.

Brown, Diana
N.D.   Umbanda: a religious movement in Brazil. (Unpublished Ms.).

Bunzel, Ruth
1952   Chichicastenango. Publication of the American Ethnological Society, XXII. New York.

Candido, Antonio
1951   The Brazilian family. *In* Brazil, Portrait of a Half Continent, edited by T. Lynn Smith and Alexander Marchant. New York, Dryden Press.

Caplow, Theodore
1952   The modern Latin American city. *In* Acculturation in the Americas, edited by Sol Tax, pp. 255–60. Proceedings of the XXIX International Congress of Americanists. Chicago, University of Chicago Press.

Cardoso, Fernando Henrique
1964   Empresário industrial e desenvolvimento econômico. São Paulo.

Carroll, Thomas
1961   The land reform issue in Latin America. *In* Latin American Issues: Essays and Comments, edited by Albert Hirshman. New York, The Twentieth Century Fund, pp. 161–201.

Centro Latino Americano de Pesquizas em Ciências Sociais
1961   Situação social da América Latina. Rio de Janeiro.

Cosio Villegas, Daniel
1963   Nationalism and development. *In* Latin American: Evolution or Explosion, edited by Mildred Adams. New York.

Costa, Esdras Borges
1955 Relaçoes de família em Cerrado e Retiro. Sociologia, XVII(2).

Crevenna, Theo R. (Editor)
1950 Materiales para el estudio de la clase media en America Latina. Washington, Unión Pan Americana. 5 vols.

Crowley, Daniel J.
1957 Plural and differential acculturation in Trinidad. American Anthropologist: 59(5) October: 817–24.

Dias, Jorge
1955 Algumas consideraçoes acêrca da estrutura social do povo português. Revista de Antropologia: III(13).

Dore, Ronald P.
1964 Latin America and Japan compared. In Continuity and Change in Latin America, edited by John J. Johnson. Stanford, Stanford University Press. pp. 227–249.

Ellison, Fred
1964 The writers. In Continuity and Change in Latin America, edited by John J. Johnson. Stanford, Stanford University Press, pp. 79–100.

Ewald, Robert H.
1957 San Antonio Sacatepequiz 1932–53. In Political Changes in Guatemalan Indian Communities, edited by Richard N. Adams. Middle American Research Institute, Tulane University.

Firth, Raymon (Editor)
1956 Studies of kinship in London. Monograph of London School of Economics.

Foster, George
1948 Empire's children: the people of Tzintzuntzan. Institute of Social Anthropology, publication 6. Washington, D.C. Smithsonian Institution.
1953 What is folk culture? American Anthropologist, 55: 159–73.

Frazier, E. Franklin
1949 The Negro in the United States. New York, Macmillan.

Freyre, Gilberto
1936 Sobrados e mucambos. Rio de Janeiro, José Olympio Editora.
1943 Casa Grande e senzala. 4th ed. Rio de Janeiro, José Olympio Editora.
1946 The masters and the slaves (Translated by Samuel Putnam). New York, Knopf.

Galvão, Eduardo
1955 Santos e visagens, um estudo da vida religiosa de Itá, Amazonas. São Paulo, Companhia Editora Nacional.

Garigue, Philip
1956 French Canadian kinship and urban life. American Anthropologist, 58(6): 1090–1101.

Germani, Gino
1962 Política y sociedad en una época de transición. Buenos Aires.

Germani, Gino, and Kalman Silvert.
1965 Estructura social e intervención militar en América Latina. In Argentina Sociedad de Massas by Torcuato S. di Tella, Gino Germani, Jorge Graciarema, and collaborators. Buenos Aires.

Gillin, John
1947a Moche: a Peruvian coastal community. Institute of Social Anthropology, No. 3. Smithsonian Institution, Washington, D.C.
1947b Modern Latin American culture. Social Forces, 25(3): 243–48. Baltimore, Md.
1949 Mestizo America. In Most of the World, edited by Ralph Linton. New York, Columbia University Press. pp. 156–211.
1951 The culture of securtiy in San Carlos: a study of a Guatemalan community of Indians and ladinos. Middle American Research Institute, Tulane University, No. 16. New Orleans.
1955 Ethos components in modern Latin American culture. American Anthropologist, LVII: 488–500.

Greenfield, Sidney
1961 Industrialization and the family in sociological theory. American Journal of Sociology, LXVII (3).
N.D. The little community and national integration: A study of patronage, power, and politics in Brazil. (Unpublished Ms.)
Guzzardi, Walter Jr.
1962 The crucial middle class. In Fortune, February.
Harris, Marvin
1952 Race relations in Minas Velhas: a community in the mountain region of Central Brazil. In Race and Class in Rural Brazil, edited by Charles Wagley. UNESCO, Paris, pp. 47–81.
1956 Town and country in Brazil. New York, Columbia University Press.
1965 Patterns of race in the Americas. New York, Walker and Co.
Henriques, Fernando
1953 Family and colour in Jamaica. London, McClelland.
Herskovits, Melville
1941 The myth of the Negro past. New York, Harpers.
Hutchinson, Carmelita Junqueira Ayres.
1955 Notas preliminares ao estudo da família no Brasil. II Reunião Brasileira de Antropólogos, Bahia.
Hutchinson, Harry William
1952 Race relations in a rural community of the Bahian Recôncavo. In Race and Class in Rural Brazil, edited by Charles Wagley. UNESCO, Paris, pp. 16–46.
1957 Village and plantation life in Northeastern Brazil. American Ethnological Society. University of Washington Press, Seattle.
Imaz, José Luis de
1964 Los que mandan. Buenos Aires. Editorial Universitária de Buenos Aires.
Johnson, John J.
1958 Political change in Latin America: the emergence of the middle class sectors. Stanford, Stanford University Press.

Kottak, Conrad
1966 The structure of equality in a Brazilian fishing community (Ph.D. dissertation, Columbia University, N.Y., Department of Anthropology). University Microfilm, Ann Arbor.

Kroeber, Alfred L.
1948 Anthropology. New York, Harcourt, Brace & Co.

La Farge, Oliver
1940 Maya ethnology: the sequence of cultures. In The Maya and Their Neighbors. New York, Appleton-Century Co., pp. 281–91.

Leeds, Anthony
1957 Economic cycles in Brazil: the persistence of a total culture pattern. (Ph.D. dissertation, Columbia University, N.Y., Department of Anthropology.) University Microfilm, Ann Arbor.

Leiris, Michel
1955 Contacts de civilization en Martinique et Guadeloupe. Paris, UNESCO.

Lewis, Oscar
1951 Life in a Mexican village. Urbana, University of Illinois Press.
1952 Urbanization without breakdown: a case study. The Scientific Monthly, 75: 31–41.
1959 Five families: Mexican case studies in the culture of poverty. New York, Basic Books.
1961 The Children of Sanchez. New York, Random House.
1966 La Vida. New York, Random House.

Linton, Ralph
1936 The study of man. New York, Appleton-Century Co.
1945 The cultural background of personality. New York, Appleton-Century Co.

Loomis, Charles, and Reed M. Powell.
1951 Class status in rural Costa Rica: a peasant community compared with a hacienda community. In Materiales para el Estudio de la Clase Media en la America Latina. Washington, D.C. Pan American Union, Vol. 5.

Mangin, William P.
1965 The role of regional associations in the adaptation of rural migrants to cities in Peru. *In* Contemporary Cultures and Societies of Latin America, edited by Dwight B. Heath and Richard N. Adams. New York, Random House, pp. 311–23.

Manners, Robert
1956 Tabara: subcultures of tobacco and mixed crops municipality. *In* The People of Puerto Rico, edited by Julian Steward. Urbana, University of Illinois Press, pp. 93–170.

McArthur, Harry S.
1961 La structura politica-religiosa de Aguacatan. Guatemala Indígena, I(2). Guatemala.

Métraux, Alfred
1951 Making a living in Marbial Valley. Paris, UNESCO.

Mintz, Sidney
1953a The folk-urban continuum and the rural proletarian community. American Journal of Sociology, LIX(2): 136–43. Chicago.

1953b The culture history of a Puerto Rican sugar cane plantation. Hispanic American Historical Review, XXXIII(2): 224–51. Durham, N.C., Duke University Press.

1956 Canamelar: the subculture of a rural sugar plantation proletariat. *In* The People of Puerto Rico, edited by Julian Steward. Urbana, University of Illinois Press, pp. 314–417.

1959 Internal market systems as mechanisms of social articulation. *In* Intermediate Societies, Social Mobility, and Communication, edited by Verne Ray. American Ethnological Society, Seattle, pp. 20–30.

Mishkin, Bernard
1946 The contemporary Quechúa. *In* Handbook of South American Indian, edited by Julian Steward, Vol. II:411–70. Bureau of American Ethnology, Bulletin 143, Smithsonian Institution, Washington, D.C.

Nash, June
1960 Protestantism in an Indian village in the Western high-

lands of Guatemala. Alpha, Kappa, Delta (Winter), pp. 49–53.

Nash, Manning
1957 Cantel 1944–54. *In* Political Changes in Guatemalan Indian Communities, edited by Richard N. Adams. Middle American Research Institute, Tulane University, New Orleans.

Nogueira, Oracy
1955 Relações raciais no município de Itapetininga. *In* Relações Raciais entre Negros e Brancos em São Paulo, edited by Florestan Fernandes and Roger Bastide. São Paulo. pp. 362–554.
1959a Preconceito racial de marca e preconceito racial de origem. Annais do XXXI Congresso Internacional de Americanistas, pp. 409–34. São Paulo.
1959b Skin color and class. *In* Plantation systems of the New World. Pan American Union, Social Science Monographs, VII: 164–87. Washington, D.C.

Padilla Seda, Elena
1956 Nocorá: the subculture of workers on a government-owned plantation. *In* People of Puerto Rico, edited by Julian Steward, Urbana, University of Illinois Press, pp. 265–313.

Patch, Richard W.
1960 Bolivia: U.S. Assistance in a revolutionary setting. *In* Social Change in Latin America Today. Council on Foreign Relations. New York, Harpers.

Pearse, Andrew
1958 Notas sobre a organização social duma favela no Rio de Janeiro. *In* Educação e Ciências Sociais. Ano 3: 9–32.

Pierson, Donald
1942 Negroes in Brazil. Chicago, University of Chicago Press. (New edition 1966.)
1952 Cruz das Almas: a Brazilian village. Institute of Social Anthropology, publication 12. Smithsonian Institution, Washington, D.C.

Pozas, Ricardo
1962 Juan, the Chamula: an ethnographic recreation of the life of a Mexican Indian. (Translated by Lysander Kemp.) Berkeley, University of California Press.

Ramos, Arthur
1944 Las poblaciones del Brasil. México.

Redfield, Robert
1941 The folkculture of Yucatán. Chicago, University of Chicago Press.
1953 The primitive world and its transformations. Ithaca, Cornell University Press.
1956 The little community. Chicago, University of Chicago Press.

Reina, Ruben E.
1960 Chinautla: a Guatemalan Indian community. Middle America Research Institute, Tulane University, New Orleans.

Rycroft, W. Stanley, and Myrtle M. Clemen.
1963 A factual study of Latin America. Office of Research, United Presbyterian Church, New York.

Scheele, Raymond
1956 The prominent families of Puerto Rico. In The People of Puerto Rico, edited by Julian Steward. Urbana, University of Illinois Press, pp. 418–62.

Service, Elman Rand, and Helen Service.
1954 Tobatí Paraguayan town. Chicago, University of Chicago Press.

Silvert, Kalman H.
1961 The conflict society: reaction and revolution in Latin America. New Orleans, The Hauser Press.
1967 The politics of social and economic change in Latin America. The Sociological Review Monograph No. 11. University of Keele [England], pp. 47–58.

Smith, T. Lynn
1946 Brazil: people and institutions. Baton Rouge, Louisiana State University.

1963   Brazil: people and institutions. Baton Rouge, Louisiana State University. 2nd edition.

Solari, Aldo E.
1964   Estudos sobre la sociedad Uruguaya. ARCA, Montevidéo.

Spiegel, Henry
1949   The Brazilian economy: chronic inflation and sporadic industrialization. Philadelphia, Blakiston Co.

Stein, William W.
1957   Outside contact and cultural stability in a Peruvian highland community. In Cultural Stability and Culture Change. American Ethnological Society, University of Washington Press, Seattle.
1961   Hualcán: life in the highlands of Peru. Cornell University Press, Ithaca.

Steward, Julian
1950   Area research: theory and practice. Social Science Research Council, Bulletin 63. New York.
1953   Culture patterns of Puerto Rico. Annals of the American Academy of Political and Social Science (January), pp. 95–102. Philadelphia.

Steward, Julian, editor
1956   The People of Puerto Rico, University of Illinois Press, Urbana.

Strickon, Arnold
1960   The grandson of the Gauchos: a study in sub-cultural persistence. (Ph.D. dissertation, Columbia University, Department of Anthropology.) University Microfilms, Ann Arbor.
1962   Class and Kinship in Argentina. Ethnology I(4).
1964   Anthropology in Latin America. In Social Science Research in Latin America, edited by Charles Wagley. New York, Columbia University Press, pp. 125–167.

Tavares de Sá, Hernane
1947   The Brazilians: people of tomorrow. New York, John Day & Co.

Tax, Sol
1953 Penny capitalism: a Guatemalan Indian economy. Institute of Social Anthropology, publication 16. Smithsonian Institution, Washington, D.C.

Taylor, Carl C.
1948 Rural life in Argentina. Baton Rouge, La State University Press.

Tschopik, Harry, Jr.
1951 The Aymará of Chucuito, Peru: I Magic. Anthropological Papers of the American Museum of Natural History, Vol. 44, pt. 2. New York.

Tumin, Melvin
1952 Caste in a peasant society. Princeton, Princeton University Press.

United Nations
1948 Economic survey of Latin America: 1948. United Nations publication.

Vidart, Daniel
1955 La vida rural Uruguayana. Montevidéo.

Villa-Rojas, Alfonso
1945 The Maya of east central Quintana Roo. Carnegie Institution of Washington, D.C., No. 559. Washington, D.C.

Wagley, Charles
1941 The economics of a Guatemalan village. American Anthropological Association Memoir 58. Menasha.

1948 Regionalism and cultural unity in Brazil. Social Forces 26:457–64. Baltimore, Md.

1949 The social and religious life of a Guatemalan village. American Anthropological Association Memoir 71. Menasha.

1953a An introduction to Latin American culture. Washington, D.C. Foreign Service Institute, Department of State.

1953b Amazon town: a study of man in the tropics. New York, The Macmillan Co. (Reprint 1964, Alfred Knopf, New York.)

224 BIBLIOGRAPHICAL REFERENCES

1955 Brazilian Community Studies: a Methodological Evaluation. *In* Annais do XXXI Congresso Internacional de Americanistas, São Paulo, 1955, pp. 357–376.

1957 Plantation America: a cultural sphere. *In* Caribbean Studies: A Symposium, edited by Vera Rubin. Institute of Social and Economic Research, University College of the West Indies, Jamaica, BWI, pp. 3–13.

1960 The Brazilian revolution: social change since 1930. *In* Social Change in Latin America Today, by Richard Adams *et al.* New York, Harpers Co., pp. 177–230.

1963 An introduction to Brazil. New York, Columbia University Press.

Wagley, Charles (Editor)
1952 Race and class in rural Brazil. Paris, UNESCO.

Wagley, Charles, and Eduardo Galvão
1949 The Tenetehara Indians of Brazil. New York, Columbia University Press.

Wagley, Charles, and Marvin Harris
1955 A typology of Latin American sub-cultures. American Anthropologist, 57 (June); 428–51.

Whetten, Nathan L.
1948 Rural Mexico. Chicago, University of Chicago Press.
1961 Guatemala: the land and the people. New Haven, Yale University Press.

Whiteford, Andrew H.
1960 Two cities of Latin America. Logan Museum Publications in Anthropology No. 9, Beloit, Wisconsin.

Whitten, N. E.
1965 Class, kinship and power in an Ecuadorian town. Stanford, Stanford University Press.

Willems, Emilio
1947 Cunha: tradição e transição em uma cultura rural do Brasil. São Paulo, Secretaria da Agricultura do Estado de São Paulo.
1953 The structure of the Brazilian Family. Social Forces 31.

Wilson, Charles
  N.D. Research in progress on Mexican factories, personal communication.
Wolf, Eric R.
  1955 Types of Latin American peasantry. American Anthropologist, 57 (June): 452–71.
  1956a San José: sub-cultures of a "traditional" coffee municipality. *In* The People of Puerto Rico, edited by Julian Steward. Urbana, University of Illinois Press, pp. 171–264.
  1956b Aspects of Group relations in a complex society: Mexico. American Anthropologist, 58 (December): 1065–78.
  1962 Review of "Chinautla: a Guatemalan Community," by Ruben Reina. American Anthropologist, 64(1) Part 1. Menasha.
Young, Michael, and Peter Wilmott
  1957 Family and kinship in east London. Glencoe, Ill., The Free Press.
Zimmerman, Ben
  1952 Race relations in the arid *sertão*. *In* Race and Class in Rural Brazil, edited by Charles Wagley. Paris, UNESCO, pp. 82–115.

INDEX

DATE DUE